Getting into the Bible

D1523158

Getting into the Bible

By
Sandy Dengler

MOODY PRESS

CHICAGO

© **1979 by**
THE MOODY BIBLE INSTITUTE
OF CHICAGO

The use of selected references from various versions
of the Bible in this publication does not necessarily
imply publisher endorsement of the versions in their
entirety.

Library of Congress Cataloging in Publication Data
Dengler, Sandy.
    Getting into the Bible.

    1. Bible—Study.   I. Title.
BS600.2.D38   220.07   79-15064
ISBN O-8024-2923-8

Second Printing, 1981

Printed in the United States of America

Contents

Chapter   **Page**

1. SETTLING IN   9
    What This Country Needs
        (Finding time)
    Serendipity's Children
        (Choosing the best study time)
    Night and Day

2. BIBLE, BIBLE, WHO'S GOT THE BIBLE?   13
    Some Nutshell History of the Scriptures
    The Old Testament
        (Genesis through Malachi)
    The New Testament
        (Matthew through Revelation)
    Babel Under Control—Sort of
        (The languages of Scripture)
    Here Comes Controversy
        (The English Bible revised)
    So What?
        (Which version should you use?)
    What's the Difference Between a Duck?
        (Paraphrases)
    Great! Now Which Edition?
        (Options concerning editions)
    Other Tools
    Colored Pencils?!
    And Most Important of All

3. THE FIRST PASS   29
    So Relax!
        (Getting comfortable with the Word)
    Use Your Imagination

4. WHY BOTHER? OR, WALKING IN THE WORD 33
Cookbooking It
Enough Already
Do as I Say, Not as I Do
Pepper-Uppers
A Word to the Hungry

5. ONCE MORE WITH FEELING 39
Peeling the Onion
(Seeking out deeper levels of meaning)
Literal or Figurative?
Perspective
(How you look at things)
Pitfalls
(Errors a Bible reader can fall into)

6. REFLECTIONS IN THE LIVING WATER 51
The Use of Cross-references
Typical Typical
(Types and shadows)

7. HELP FOR THE SYMBOL—MINDED 57

8. HELP! HELP! 61
Commentary
Concordance
Topical Bible
Bible Dictionary
Atlas
Greek and Hebrew Lexicons
Other Aids

9. NOW THAT YOU'VE GOT IT 67
The Mind of God
The Mind of Christ

Duty
Purpose
Personal Guidance
Cross-fertilization
Moving Right Along
     (Starting out in the New Testa-
     ment; avoiding bogging down)
The Last Page

APPENDIX A:
     BACKGROUND ON THE BIBLE'S BOOKS 74

APPENDIX B:
     THE CHRONOLOGY OF SCRIPTURE   103

1

SETTLING IN

As a new Christian or perhaps a renewed believer, you've noticed this by now: we older Christians have all sorts of advice for you. Among other things, we assure you that you must get deep into serious Bible study right away.

Right!

But how?

How can you know you aren't being led into false doctrine by some cult when you know very little about the Bible—yet? How can you be sure the study guide or leader is straight in the Scripture? And the Bible is so, so deep. And thick. Almost scary.

The purpose of this guide is to help you mine the gold of Scripture on your own. It won't be long before you'll want to try correspondence study (there are some splendid mail-order studies), group Bible study, maybe even formal classroom instruction.

But for now, you are just getting started. If you feel afraid, talk yourself out of it. Exploring Scripture isn't work—it's high adventure! If you feel wary, good! Along with the pure gold of God's Word there is a lot of counterfeit in the world. The Christian does well to be cautious. Your measure is the Scripture itself. In God's Word is a solid ruler with which to measure everything that is written about Jesus and the Bible.

And so, as you begin with the three essential ingredi-
ents—you, your Bible, and the Holy Spirit as your teacher,
God bless you with fruitful study!

What This Country Needs
(Is a Good Twenty-five Hour Day)

You've already figured this out: The most important part
of Bible study is getting started. It is also the hardest part.
And the next hardest part is sticking with it.

Wouldn't a twenty-five-hour day be nifty? Not really. We
all have something that would fill that other hour already.
You are just going to have to gouge some study time out of
the existing twenty-four-hour day. There are two ways to
set up study time.

• Rearrange your day so that you fill up the little unused
holes in your schedule—fifteen minutes here, half an hour
there. We spend lots of hours on things that are less important than God's Word.

• Or, substitute an hour of study for an hour of
something else. If that something else is a thing you really
enjoy (an extra hour of sleep or a favorite TV show), chalk
off the substitution as "sacrificial living." For that is exactly
what "making a sacrifice" means.

Serendipity's Children

Serendipity is the knack of stumbling upon some interesting thing in an offhand, casual manner—finding when
you didn't realize you were seeking. Some people are
always well organized, doing their seeking in a methodical
and orderly way. But lots of us must depend upon serendipity.

If you thrive on a routine where study time is set neatly
aside each day, every day, you are fantastic! Hats off to
you! Seek and ye shall find.

Too bad, but not every kind of personality lends itself to

a regular schedule. Some folks flit through the day like a jackrabbit in a cactus patch, leaping here and there, pausing, turning. If it weren't for serendipity they wouldn't find anything at all.

When such a person binds himself to a schedule and then can't stick to it, guilt and frustration take over. Bible study should be serious, but never a guilt trip.

If you can make a daily reading schedule work, by all means use it. For this is the best way. But if you cannot, set up a more casual system. Keep your Bible out in an obvious place where you see it all the time. Keep it with your car keys. Set it on your coffee mug.

If you spend four hours on Monday and don't touch your Bible again until Thursday, you still average an hour a day. Keep a calendar record of time spent in study so that you don't shortchange yourself on study time. Use bits and parcels of time (waiting for the kids at the dentist's; the hour between Favorite Show #1 and Favorite Show #2, when you used to watch TV but weren't interested). The more you pick up your Bible, the more you get into the Word, the easier it will be.

Night and Day

Night people and day people. Night people are in a fog until noon and do their best stuff after 9:00 P.M. Day people are up, all bright eyed, at some miserable hour of the morning (it wouldn't be so bad if they weren't so smug about cracking dawn). And whichever you are, your roommate and/or spouse is just the opposite, right?

The night person should try to get into his Bible late in the day, when learning is at its best. A day person is sharpest in the morning and should therefore crack his Bible early. Both give the best time of their day to study. Watch your patterns. Choose the study time that will reap the richest benefits.

2

BIBLE, BIBLE,

WHO'S GOT THE BIBLE?

Every Christian has a favorite version. "This is best!" says one. "No, that one is best, because—" claims another. And you don't know the differences between any of them. How do you choose the version that is best for you? Before choosing, let's see how all these versions came to be.

Some Nutshell History of the Scriptures

"Solomon in all his glory." "King Solomon's mines." Solomon ruled in Israel around 1000 B.C. Other kings and nations may have been wealthier, dollar for dollar, but such comparisons are just a paper exercise. Surfeit is surfeit. The little kingdom of Israel in its glory was splendid beyond desire.

Israel's national literature was splendid, too. Some books wore a gentle patina of age measured in millennia. Other works were brand new, written by the kings themselves. Some of the literature would eventually become parts of the Old Testament.

But around 600 B.C. the splendor faded. Jerusalem and its magnificent Temple were torn down by invaders. The

Hebrews were starved, butchered, enslaved, and exiled. Israel was dead. Nothing was left.

After seventy years as slaves in Babylon, a very few Hebrews returned home. They rebuilt the Temple, but it was not so wonderful as the first Temple had been. Jerusalem became a city again. And the literature survived.

For the next five hundred years Israel would belong to one empire after another. The Medes and Persians took it away from Babylon. Alexander the Great conquered the Persians (around 300 B.C.), and Israel was a Greek province. About 167 B.C. the Jews revolted and became an independent nation for a short time. But in 63 B.C. Pompey the Great conquered Israel in the name of Rome. Rome still owned it when Jesus was born.

But the Jews were a troublesome lot, not good Roman subjects at all. Their literature promised them independence, milk and honey. And they wanted it *now!* Fed up with the constant grumbling and piecemeal insurrections, Rome sent General Titus out to Jerusalem with a torch. In A.D. 70 he burned Jerusalem and sold so many Hebrews into slavery that the slave market was glutted. The last Jewish nationalists, holed up in the fastness of Masada, were destroyed a year or so later.

The land was desolate again, just as the Hebrew literature had promised. The Jews were scattered all over the world, without a home of their own, as the ancient writings had predicted. As far as the world was concerned, Israel was gone forever.

The Old Testament (Genesis through Malachi)

The first part of the Old Testament was already ancient literature when Solomon ruled. Kings, prophets, and historians added to the literature until about 400 B.C., when it became apparent that God no longer spoke through prophets. Some of this literature had always been recognized as being of God. Other was secular but still considered accurate (for example, in 2 Chronicles the reader is referred to other reference books, as in 25:26, 27:7, 32:32). Some writings were in between, doubtful. Did they carry the full authority of God, or did they not?

The literature universally recognized by Jewish scholars as being from God is our Old Testament. *Canon* is the word scholars use—it means those books assigned the special rank of bearing God's full authority, His Word without error. Esther was included in this canon over some protest (the book does not, for instance, ever mention the name of God). Song of Solomon was almost not included—too lusty. Maccabbees and certain other historical works were left out of the canon—the special group of inspired works—but were saved separately as accurate history.

This canon business raises a serious question. How can we be sure those scholars made 100 percent correct choices? Was something left out? Perhaps something was included in Holy Scripture that shouldn't be there. How do we know those Jewish scholars assembled the Old Testament exactly the way God wants it?

Our guide in this matter (as in all matters) is Jesus. Since we are believers, when Jesus says something, we believe Him. When Jesus said, "Thy word is truth," in John 17:17, He was referring to the Old Testament. The Old Testament is commonly called the Word (as in Psalm 119), among other terms. In every discourse where Jesus quoted Old Testament Scripture, He gave it full authority. He even built a whole theological argument on the tense of the verb "to be" (Matthew 22:31-32).

Paul, writing in the Spirit, also gave full authority to the Old Testament, the same Old Testament we have today

(2 Timothy 3:16, for instance). Because Jesus, as well as His servants and apostles, had total confidence in the Old Testament, we can also.

The New Testament (Matthew through Revelation)

Before the clouds of the ascension had drifted away, men were busy writing about Jesus Christ. (Incidentally, it is not true that Jesus was illiterate. He opened His public ministry by reading aloud in the synagogue at Nazareth, Luke 4:16-21).

Paul and James wrote letters that were circulating in the churches before A.D. 50. Conservative scholars suggest these probable dates for the Gospels:

- Mark, around A.D. 50.
- Matthew, around A.D. 56 to 58.
- Luke, around A.D. 58 to 60 but before A.D. 63
- John, perhaps A.D. 90 or 95.

(For comparison, Jesus was probably born about 4 B.C. and was crucified about A.D. 30).

Somewhere around A.D. 150 a writer named Tatian took the four authoritative gospels (the ones accepted as gospel in both his day and ours) and constructed the first harmony (a harmony rearranges the gospel narratives into chronological order). The fact that Tatian chose Matthew, Mark, Luke, and John shows that the earliest Christian writers respected those gospels as being accurate.

Peter claimed that Paul's writings had just as much authority as the Old Testament itself (2 Peter 3:16).

Like the Jews, the Christians established a canon. That is, they gathered together into one book (the New Testament) writings that they were sure had come directly from God. Some three hundred years after Jesus, church leaders met and decided which of the many writings were holy.

They agreed squarely on the books that are our New Testament. They agreed that certain letters and essays were popular but not truly inspired. These were left out. And there was a chunk of fourteen books and letters called the Apocrypha about which there was some doubt.

Are the Apocrypha to be included in the canon? The question hung in limbo for centuries until the church split into Catholic and Protestant factions. The Protestants decided no, as had the Jews. The Apocrypha are not canonical. The Papal Christians hopped off onto the other side of the fence. Yes, they are too. And so the question rests today. The Catholic Bibles include the Apocrypha. The Protestant Scriptures do not. Otherwise, they are just alike. Both Bibles agree on the other sixty-six books.

Here's that question again. How can we be sure the New Testament is exclusively the Word of God? How can we be certain those Christian scholars didn't make any errors when they picked out the books for the canon?

Jesus in the flesh had come and gone before the New Testament was written. So of course He couldn't quote from it or testify to it. So He sent us the Holy Spirit (John 16:7-15) as a teacher and guide. The church leaders evoked this Counselor when they put together the canon. It is the Holy Spirit's job to supervise a situation of this sort. And we can be certain that the Holy Spirit did His job.

As for the gospels that tell about Jesus, they were all accepted as genuine from the very beginning. This means that people who were alive when Jesus walked the Holy Land were still alive when the gospels were written. Any myths or false claims would have been denied by people who knew Jesus firsthand. Indeed, many phony works were exposed that way. But the gospels have stood. Besides—would all those martyrs have died to defend a lie?

We have another assurance. Pretend that some books were accidentally left out—or mistakenly included (not true, of course—we're pretending). The basic facts about our faith are not founded on one solitary passage somewhere in a single book. They are built upon the foundation of Christ Himself and are found in many places. If some books were removed, or included, the basic facts of the faith would still remain unchanged.

Babel Under Control—Sort Of

Alexander the Great (about 300 B.C.) was not a generous man. But he gave the Mediterranean world a splendid gift—a common language. As he built his Greek Empire, common Greek (called *Koine*) became the everyday language all over. Barbarian and scholar, farmer and pirate all knew what we today might call "business Greek."

Since 600 B.C. the Jews had been spattered like birdshot over all the civilized world. They learned Greek along with everyone else and also picked up the language of the Gentiles (non-Jews, that is) around them. In fact, they seemed to be losing their native Hebrew. Many Jews could not read their own Scriptures.

So a group of linguists (tradition says seventy of them) got together in Alexandria, Egypt, around 250 B.C. They translated parts of the Old Testament from Hebrew into Greek. Over the next two centuries, the rest of Hebrew Scripture was put into Greek. This translation, called the Septuagint, is still in use. In fact, Jesus knew it and quoted from it most of the time.

This was a heavy thing to the Jews, their Scriptures in Greek. From the beginning they had been very, very careful to preserve the Word without an error. They used all sorts of tricks—counting columns, letters, words, and dots—to prevent errors from sneaking in as copies were made.

The Septuagint, though, was so popular it threatened to become the only version of the Jews' Scriptures. So another group of scholars, called the Masoretes, made a careful, authoritative text in Hebrew. For it, they gathered up all the ancient books they could find in the nations of exile. How close to the originals did they come? Modern Hebrew text, the Masoretic text, and texts from before 100 B.C. all show *no significant differences.*

Alexander the Great had made the Mediterranean a Greek sea. Now General Pompey, in the sixties B.C., made it a Roman lake. But although the old Greek Empire was now an expanded Roman Empire, Latin never caught on the way Greek had. Everyday people still spoke Greek. At the time Jesus lived, you spoke Hebrew to your dear old mother, haggled with merchants or talked to your Idumean girl friend in Greek, and paid taxes in Latin. When Pilate ordered the sign nailed to Jesus' cross, it had to be in three languages (Luke 23:38). Hebrew was the local language of Judea; Greek was the language everybody knew; and Latin was the official state language of Rome, the conqueror.

Although Matthew did some writing in his native Aramaic (related to Hebrew), he and all other New Testament writers did their work in Greek. What a blessing that was! Now both the Old and New Testaments could circulate freely all over the Mediterranean world with absolutely no language barriers to buck. People throughout Western civilization could read the Bible without having to translate.

In the early three hundreds A.D., the Emperor, Constantine, made Christianity respectable. The official state religion adopted the official state language. Around A.D. 400 the Scriptures were translated from Greek into Latin. The translator, Jerome, did his work so well that his ver-

sion, the Latin Vulgate, is still the official version of the
Roman church fifteen hundred years later.

Churches and universities used Latin and Greek. But
the peasants no longer spoke Greek and never did learn
Latin. By A.D. 1100 the Bible was available in French.
Within two hundred years the Bible could also be read in
English, German, and Italian.

At first, church leaders objected to the Holy Bible in
common languages. They got over it. By 1604, James I of
England saw the need for an official Bible in English. So he
appointed fifty-four scholars to make one. Their translation, officially called the Authorized Version (AV) and
unofficially called the King James Version (KJV), has been
the English Bible for over three hundred years.

Here Comes Controversy

Over those three hundred years the King James Version
stayed the same. But English changed. "Suffer" no longer
means "allow." "Prevent" is no longer "go before." Around
1870 (right after the American Civil War), scholars in
England got together to revise the King James—to modern-
ize it. While they were at it, they also modernized the old
Greek text on which the translation was based.

The new Greek text became the center of a mighty
brouhaha. Supporters of the new text said:

• The new text is based upon the very oldest
manuscripts—writings the King James translators hadn't
known about.

• The modern scholars represent the very best in
scholarship.

• The new text eliminates little errors that had happened over centuries of copying and therefore is closer to
the original (called an autograph) than is the Stephens
1550 Greek text that the KJV translators used.

Hmmph! say the supporters of the old 1550 Greek text.

On the contrary, they say:

• The committee in 1870 had no business monkeying around with the Greek in the first place. Their only job was to prepare an English version.

• The new text is based on old manuscripts, all right. They were inferior, and therefore not used, four hundred years ago, and they are still inferior. In fact, some of those manuscripts were altered by early heretics in the church.

• There wasn't a thing wrong with the scholarship of the King James translators. Indeed, their theology was more conservative than that of the new translators.

• Most of the so-called corrections in the new Greek version concern the person of Jesus Christ and tend to reduce His deity. Therefore the 1550 text is to be preferred as the received text (that is, the text received from God via the Holy Spirit).

So What?

Today, the King James Version is the only widely used version based on the older Stephens 1550 Greek text, the text conservative scholars prefer. (The Douay-Confraternity Version is also, but that one is now out of print.) The modern versions all pretty much depend upon the new text, called Westcott-Hort.

Why read the King James? You will find the well-worded modern versions much easier to read and understand. They don't sound preachy or vague. But on the other hand, you should be reading the King James because:

• Most reference books you will use later— concordances, dictionaries, and so on—are based upon the King James.

• Certain facts and phrases found only in the 1550 Greek text will be lost to you if you do not read the King James.

• A lot of people memorize their favorite passages from the King James. You should be familiar with it because most others are also.

The solution sounds like a cop-out. It is not. Read two versions—the King James and also a modern one. It is more than worth the extra effort! Why, that in itself will multiply your insight into Scripture.

Now, Which Version? Conservative Bible scholars disagree on which modern versions are "worst" and which "best." Basically the differences reflect certain passages that omit words, passages reduced to footnotes, or certain words translated differently. For instance:

• Is "begotten" omitted in John 3:16?

• Is the word in Isaiah 7:14 translated as "virgin" or "young woman" (conservative scholars prefer "virgin")?

• Are John 7:53-8:11 and Mark 16:9-19 kept in the text, or are they reduced to footnotes?

There is a long list of such criteria.

Another important factor to consider when choosing a version is that nearly all the major reference works are based on the King James. Concordances, dictionaries, and the classic commentaries all catalog King James words. Therefore it is wise to choose a version that follows King James vocabulary and phrases closely. When you get into the heavy reference stuff—especially concordances—you can find the passages you want with a minimum of hassle.

For example: The *New American Standard Bible* (NASB) uses a lot of phrases and words from the King James. On the other hand, the Jerusalem Bible is just as scholarly a translation, but it is worded in such a way that traditional research books are almost useless.

In any event, avoid cult-written versions. In places they may be adjusted to conform to a preconceived theology. The translators may be perfectly sincere, but that does not make their works correct. If a truth is a truth, it will be clear in any honest, scholastically correct translation.

What's the Difference Between a Duck?

One of the most popular Bibles on the market today is not a translation in the strict sense of the word. It is a paraphrase (this is the *Living Bible* by Kenneth Taylor). There are other well-done paraphrases also.

So what's the difference? In converting an idea or a concept from one language into another, the strict translator sticks as closely as he can to the exact words and phrases of the original language. On the other hand, the paraphraser can insert explanations, change words and phrases, rearrange whole sentences—in general, mess around quite freely. For example, the paraphraser of a heavy government treatise on national park management might want to boil down "Park Rangers Specializing in Law Enforcement" to "Tree Fuzz." The paraphraser modernizing Shakespeare's *Julius Caesar* might change "Friends! Romans! Countrymen!" into "Hey, you guys!"

Paraphrases make excellent commentaries. They change outdated or stilted-sounding phrases into good old twentieth-century language. The problem with paraphrases is that they are not exact. They reflect the paraphraser's opinion and the paraphraser, being human, makes mistakes. A paraphrase is fine for light reading. But for study, read a good, solid translation.

Great! Now Which Edition?

"I thought we just went through all that," you say.

"No. We were talking about versions," I reply.

A version is the translation. An edition is the book itself—pages, print and binding—that you hold in your hand, the thing you drop on your foot. There is a bewildering choice of editions. Here are your options:

The binding. Besides paperback, leather, and hardback, Bibles come in wide-margin editions so you can make notes around the edges, looseleaf editions in a binder so you can add notebook pages (these lie flat nicely), and even ironclad Testaments made bulletproof for gifts to servicemen.

Red-letter. This means that all the words Jesus spoke are printed in red ink.

Content. Bible versus Testament. When an edition says "Bible" this commonly means both Old and New Testaments. "Testament" means one of the two books only, usually the New Testament. Some Testaments come with Psalms and Proverbs bound in also.

"Text editions" are simplest. They contain the Bible only. Period.

"Reference editions" feature cross-references at the bottom, along the sides, or down a center column. These references will become more and more useful as you grow in the Word.

Most "student editions" have a handy set of maps in back, possibly a concordance (limited value), or a dictionary. Some include summaries of the books of the Bible, and other commentaries.

In addition to these features, "study Bibles" (such as the *Ryrie* or *Scofield*) provide cross-references, background information, and explanatory comments.

You will eventually buy a separate concordance whether your Bible has one bound in or not.

Parallel editions. These are Bibles with two or more different versions in the same book. Usually the print is arranged so that the same passage can be read in all the different versions on the same page. Nearly all such editions make the King James the first column. Next to that KJV column will be a modern version (or paraphrase) in a matching column. Most parallels treat only the New Testament, because of bulk. A popular four-parallel version of the whole Bible weighs nearly ten pounds!

Sturdiness and comfort. Your working Bible is really going to be used—noted, marked, dragged on camping trips, stuffed in your bag. You need a rugged edition (not necessarily expensive—just indestructible).

Consider the print size. Avoid small pocket-sized Bibles with teensy-weensy print. Try out a large edition with large, clear print (you can also get Bibles with oversize print for especially easy reading).

Save the treasured family heirloom for special occasions. Your working Bible will get battered.

Other Tools

Most books about Bible study urge you to buy and use a notebook. It's a great idea. Try it. But don't think you are doing something wrong if you find yourself never taking notes. A lot of people, especially when they are just beginning in Scripture, don't make many notes. And they hardly ever go back to read notes they made before.

After you've gotten into this a little way, you'll find yourself writing things down on scraps of paper that end up as bookmarks. Then is the time to think about a notebook. Leave the first two pages of the notebook blank and number the rest consecutively. When you write down ideas and notes on a topic, write the topic title on the front page along with the page number of your notes. That way you can find it again easily.

If your working Bible has one of those Family Records sections, cut the record pages out about half an inch from the spine. Glue or tape typing paper to the page stubs. You now have notebook pages bound right in. Glue more blank pages into the front and back, too.

What you will use most are colored pencils.

Colored Pencils?!

There are two reasons for coloring sentences. One, the color reminds you, the next time you read the passage, what you thought of the time before. Also, color-coding makes passages easier to find. For instance, you may remember that a certain reference to the Messiah is somewhere in Isaiah. If you have marked Messianic passages with blue, you thumb through Isaiah, checking out all blue passages. You'll find it.

Felt-tip markers bleed through the paper. Crayons smear. Use colored pencils. Get a big box with eight or twelve colors and keep it for Bible study—no other use. Neither a borrower nor a lender be with the kids. These are yours. Use a ballpoint pen or pencil for marginal notes (soft lead pencils smear and rub faint).

Start out with two or three basic colors to represent basic ideas (perhaps you may wish to use symbolic colors; see the following list). Add colors as you feel the need.

Below is not a list for you to copy. It is an example of a system that works. Set up your own system based on your own ideas and interests. You end up with more topics than colors? No problem. Just try not to make two very similar topics the same color.

- dark blue   creation; rebirth; work of Holy Spirit
- turquoise   nature of Jesus (mostly N.T.); Messianic prophecy
- dark green   prayer; worship
- light green   guidance; faith
- yellow   fulfillment of the Law; God's promises; prophecies other than Messianic

- orange   proper conduct, good behavior; duties; what God expects from us

- pink   non-Messianic prophecies that have been fulfilled; their fulfillment

- red   Satan; sin; repentance

- purple   judgment; second coming; book of life

- brown   astrology; the occult; demons

- black   wisdom; things known only to God

And Most Important of All

That's about it. You need only one other thing, and it is the most important thing of all—spiritual insight. Without it you can see only the surface of God's Word. The depths are forever hidden from you.

You see, the Bible is two books. One is a lofty, lovely collection of history and literature. The other is the mind of God. Anyone can appreciate the literature. But only the spiritually-alive person can see spiritual facts—truths. Paul explains this in 1 Corinthians 2:10-16.

If you have made a sincere commitment to Jesus Christ, you have a spiritual nature within you that will be able to see spiritual truths. You are a spiritual baby, ready to be fed on the Word and grow. If you have not made that important commitment, take that first step now.

- Admit to God that you are a sinner (ever do something the Bible says not to? Then you qualify).
- Accept that God's Son Jesus removes all sin from you. (You may not understand yet. Step out on faith and accept it. You'll understand soon.)
- Ask Jesus to become the executive director of your life. And mean it.

• Ask the Holy Spirit to help you see what you need as you study. This is His work, and He will do it. You are now a child of God, paid for with the blood of Christ, though you'll understand better soon. The depths of Scripture are yours.

All in order?

Dig in!

3

The First Pass

Of course it is wrong to regard the Scriptures lightly—to laugh or ridicule. But it is equally distressing to read them under a gloomy cloud of "All right, children. Let's get very sober and solemn." Here is God's love letter to you, personally. You will find songs, stories, one-liners, letters, legal documents, and puns.

Soon you will know the styles of the different writers. You'll like John's wonderful way with common words, Joel's gloomy word-pictures, Solomon's sensuous love poem.

As time goes on you will see how each book fits its author perfectly. David, a man of action and romance, would have a hard time with doctrinal explanations. And yet he understood the doctrine. Just look at his psalms. He sang his theology.

Matthew, a tax collector, uses words about money that you find nowhere else in Scripture. Luke, the physician, lets his medical knowledge show through here and there. All these writers wrote over a space of two thousand years. And yet they created a perfectly integrated single book with a single message throughout.

As you read, God's face will shine like a diamond, one facet after another. At first some facets will seem to face in opposite directions. They will sound like contradictions. God is too big to fit into one little facet. But He is one whole, and all His many sides will show themselves to you as you grow spiritually.

So Relax!

If you read best draped across an overstuffed chair, drape yourself. The first pass is a get-acquainted thing. So read your passage once through just to enjoy it.

You'll miss a lot of things the first time through. Don't worry. You'll keep the names and people straight as they become more real—as they come alive.

And those names! You can skip over them, or you can work them out. Skipping is the chicken way out. Say the name out loud. Pencil in pronunciation marks. It will pay off when someone asks you to read out loud during a group Bible study.

But more important, as you say those goofy-sounding names, they lose their goofiness. You won't name a child Elkanah or Mephibosheth (will you?). But those were real people once. They may even have had nicknames.

Bible characters are not stage puppets. Every person in the Bible was just like you—a human with complex needs, wants, fears, and shortcomings. The Bible has to get a lot into a little space. So it glosses over emotions and high drama. You have to fill in those emotions as you read. Think about the people. In fact, forget those Bible stories you heard as a child. You are reading adult-level stuff now.

What was going through David's mind as he stepped out in front of Goliath? He was confident. But the battle was not yet won. Goliath certainly didn't know what was coming. How was Goliath treated back in camp at night?

Q. What do you give a Bengal tiger?

A. Anything he wants, anything at all.

Same with Goliath, I'll bet.

What you already know can rob the Bible of its drama. You know what's coming, but the people in the story don't. For instance: A flock of people—thousands of them—are listening to Jesus. They haven't eaten all day. He asks them to sit in groups of fifty. As they watch Him out there across the meadow, they see that He has a handful of bread and fish—enough for maybe seven or eight people. They don't realize what He's up to, but you do. So stop.

Use Your Imagination

Pretend you're one of the five thousand, somebody at the back of the crowd. Jesus blesses the food. He starts passing it around. Fat chance you'll get any, but the stuff keeps coming. Suddenly everyone including you is full, and there are enough leftovers to feed another army. Oh, wow! Praise the holy God! How did—? Praise God!

Stop to think about the tensions and rivalries in Genesis 29, 30, and 35. No wonder Jacob mourned Joseph so bitterly and clung so tightly to Benjamin. Benjamin was all he had left from life with his beloved Rachel.

It may seem you are not getting any solid stuff. You are reading the Bible as if it were a Gothic romance. But you are getting something. You are laying a solid foundation for further study. Just as important, the Bible and its people are coming to life for you. The more personal the Bible becomes, the more you will understand from it, both now and later.

Some passages stump the experts. God is so high above us He can't get all His information to us in a way we can understand. So if you slide past some things, don't worry. After all, a first-grader just learning addition would be swamped if you dumped multiplication on him. Two years later the multiplication facts will come easily. In the same way you would be swamped if the whole meaning of every Bible passage were dumped on you all at once.

Keep your colored pencils handy (write your color system on the inside cover because you'll forget it at first). After several readings, your Bible will look like an explosion in a paint factory. "How did that get past me before?"

The bottomless depths of Scripture are one of its constant joys.

4

WHY BOTHER?
or,
WALKING IN THE WORD

After you've read the Bible, what do you do for encores?* In fact, why did you bother to wade clear through it in the first place? Is there a reason?

You bet! Lots of them.

The biggest reason, mentioned elsewhere, is to get to know God better. The more you discern the mind of God (and simultaneously, that of Jesus), the better you can serve your Lord. It is easier to get done what the Boss needs done if you know how He ticks. Every secretary knows that. It especially helps when the Boss personally gives you guidelines on how to do it. Well, that's the Bible.

In addition, the Bible spells out a life-style that's impossible to beat. Even if you weren't a Christian, you couldn't do better than to follow the Bible's teaching as a life-style. The Scriptural way of getting through life seems to pose the least hassles. Crime pays—until you get caught. Cheating works—until they catch onto you. A little white

*You already know the answer to that one—read it again.

33

lie can get you smoothly out of a sticky situation; it may also turn around and bite you unexpectedly.

But you are a Christian. So it's even more important that you lead a Scriptural (that is, a godly) life. In the first place, it pleases God (and with a first place like that, who needs a second place?). Second, the unsaved world is watching you closely, eyes narrowed and fingers ready to point derisively. You are on stage every moment. You are an ambassador for Christ (that's not my line—it's Paul's in 2 Corinthians 5:20). Your way of life is itself your greatest, most telling testimony. You can preach Jesus all day, but if you don't live Jesus, your actions will drown out your noble words.

For starters, then, there are three dandy reasons for reading the Bible and then putting it to work: (1) to know better the mind of God, (2) to know what God wants done and how He wants you to do it, and (3) to pursue the highest quality life-style possible. You are worthy of nothing less than the best!

And now the bottom line—just how do you get all this out of the Scriptures on your own?

Cookbooking It

Some rules of life are commandments, plain and simple, direct from God. The Ten Commandments (Exodus 20) are a good example. So are the pronouncements of Jesus. In fact, think of Jesus as talking to you personally as you read His words to believers in John 15 and 16, for instance.

But most of the basic guidelines need some interpretation on your part. This is only right and proper. After all, you are unique among the several billions of people on this planet. Through the Bible God is speaking personally to little old one-of-a-kind you. "Interpreting," of course, doesn't mean "bending" the rules. It means fitting them to you.

An example of such a basic guideline is Paul's instruction in 2 Corinthians 6:14: Do not become mismated (some translations say mismatched) with unbelievers. Most Christians take that to mean a Christian should never marry a non-Christian. Some believers, however, extend that guideline to include everything from granges to labor unions. They refuse, often at great cost, to hold membership in any organization at all that does not profess Christ.

Cookbooking it this way presents certain problems as well as freedoms. Brother Joe may be under enormous conviction on a point that doesn't bother you a bit. Romans 14 says don't argue with Joe. Make sure you are in God's will, don't do anything to hinder Joe's growth, and keep a close eye on your own walk.

Especially touchy (and at times divisive) is the kind of guideline that emerges from some Bible truth that is not a rule itself. F'rinstance: There is no direct commandment "Thou shalt not smoke tobacco" (which figures; until the first European explorers of the New World fetched some of the weed home, along with birds and Indians and gold, no one had ever heard of the stuff). But the Christian's body is referred to in Scripture as the temple of the Spirit (e.g., 1 Corinthians 3:16-17 and 6:19). And if this is where God's Spirit dwells, the Christian had better take good care of it. Smoking is not taking good care of the body. And this isn't even to mention that smoking wastes money that would better be spent otherwise.

That brings up another aspect to consider when you are looking for no-no's, yes-yes's, and other guidelines. It might be called "opening the door to temptation." That is, some little weakness might pave the way to a greater weakness either your own base nature or Satan can exploit for devious purposes.

An example of that sort of thing is the booze question.

Here's another guideline Christians are divided on.
Nowhere does Scripture flat-out say, "Stay away from
alcoholic beverages." Jesus did work His first miracle at
Cana by turning water into wine at a wedding. And
drinkers just love to quote 1 Timothy 5:23, wherein they
are invited to take a little wine for Timothy's stomach's
sake.

BUT! say many Christians. There are dozens of Bible
references that forbid drunkenness. A little alcohol dulls a
little. It throws wide open the doors to all sorts of temp-
tations in addition to the temptation to drink too much
booze. And it sets a terrible example for others. Thus,
while alcohol itself is not forbidden, many Christians avoid
problems by abstaining completely.

The example you set your Christian brother is no small
matter. In Romans 14, 1 Corinthians 8, and other places,
you are given a heavy responsibility to help your brother
grow. You are, in a large sense, your brother's keeper.

Enough Already!

Some Christians make a big issue out of which
guidelines (especially in the Old Testament) are for
Christians and which were meant only for Jews. Then
there are a few Christian groups who claim all the
guidelines in both testaments (except sacrifices; Jesus'
sacrifice satisfied that need). Others say everything in the
Pentateuch and so on was only to separate the Jews from
their nasty neighbors (Leviticus 18:24-30) and is of no use
to us today. And yet, you can't do any better than to take
to heart the guidelines of, say, Leviticus 19.

So how far do you go with this business? It sounds like a
heavy trip indeed, following all those rules and no-no's.
When, if at all, can you safely say, "Enough!"? Try this for a
helpful rule of thumb: Assume Jesus is looking over your
shoulder. He is, you know. Now glance at His face. Is He

smiling, yawning, sad, or ready to swat you one? He's no killjoy. He just wants you to have the best. Be happy He cares so much and cooperate.

Do as I Say, Not as I Do

The Bible has much to teach you by way of example. Jesus used the device all the time, as in His story of the good Samaritan. A lot of Old Testament stories, interesting in themselves, provide helpful advice. Take the story about King David in 2 Samuel 6:1-15 and 1 Chronicles 13 and 15. Twenty years earlier, the Philistines had swiped the sacred Ark of the Covenant and hauled it home to Philistia. When plagues and terrors befell them they unloaded it in a hurry, sending it back to Israel in a cart drawn by two cows. For years the Ark had languished on the Israeli-Philistine border. Now David was going to bring it to its rightful place in the capital city.

Since the cart and cows idea had worked just fine for the Philistines, David was using it, too. Everything seemed peachy until, halfway back, the whole happy parade was stopped cold when lightning from Heaven struck a man dead. David was, to put it mildly, bent out of shape at God. Then he did what he should have done in the first place. He turned to the Scriptures. There it was in black and white—The Ark should be carried by six Levites, not two cows. David called out a half dozen Levites and tried again. Success! The example is clearly given. The message you derive on your own. That's why God gave you that fantastic brain in the first place.

Pepper-Uppers

Another reason for reading the Bible is simply for your own personal benefit. One of the dandiest ways to build yourself up is to watch for God's promises as you read. It will be very helpful if you choose some sunny color from your pencil pack and color all the promises you find (remember that a promise of punishment for misbehavior is a promise nonetheless—and behave accordingly!). For openers, consider just three of Jesus' many promises: in Matthew 28:20, John 14:1-3, and Hebrews 13:5.

Then there are all those mood-lifters. When David felt down-and-out, he wrote a psalm. His psalms reveal a man who was really in the pits. When you feel that way yourself, it's a comfort to read them and know you're not alone. You don't have to be depressed to appreciate mood-lifters. Sometime when you're really feeling good, look up some praise passages in a concordance. You'll feel even better.

Skipping about in Scripture to fit a mood is helpful, but remember that this is not concentrated study. Hunt and peck helps you through a typing project—eventually—but it doesn't make good Bible study. Stick to systematic reading and go to special sections for special needs in addition to regular study.

A Word To The Hungry

Jesus The Word is also the Bread of Life. You must feed the spiritual you regularly even as you feed the physical you. Though the adult body must slack off on the calorie intake (the fatter the slacker), the spiritual you can never get too much Bread. When it comes to growth and maturity in your Christian walk, the more the better. So feast and enjoy!

5

ONCE MORE WITH FEELING

OK. Sit up. It's time to switch from casual reading to careful study. Perhaps you waded through the begats. You soared joyously with the psalmist. Paul's letters have just invited you to stronger discipline. John's Revelation is still swirling around your ears in vivid confusion. You have the feel of the passage. Now you are ready to dig for deeper spiritual meanings.

An excellent film or play speaks to many levels at once. At the base level is the story itself, which largely entertains. But a deeper meaning might reveal a struggle between moral and immoral urges. It may be a story of psychological desperation much deeper than the story says on the surface. The viewer may say, "I know what that character is thinking. I've been there myself."

What the viewer sees—and how much—depends on his own background. The more experiences, the broader the background, the more he can appreciate the themes and deep subtleties of the film or play.

Also, the film or play should be seen in its entirety—the whole message, the whole impression. Cutting mutilates it.

And it is exactly that way with the Bible. The Bible speaks on many levels at once. There is the surface story. There are deeper meanings and underlying themes. Which ones you see depend very much on your education and background. Every person relates differently to the Bible because no two people have the same experiences. Thus, group Bible study can be very productive when every person chips in. Everyone benefits from everyone else's background. You may not see the same things I do. I may be impressed by a passage that you think is ho-hum. That's natural. The Bible says the Holy Spirit deals with every person individually, one on one (1 Corinthians 12:11).

Peeling the Onion

Peeling an onion isn't difficult—the difficult part is knowing when to stop. You strip away the tough outer layers. And there's another layer, and waiting beneath that, still another. The onion may have been dirty on the outside—if mold has started, it may have blue gray gunk between the outer layers. But the closer you get to the center, the cleaner, more oniony your onion is.

The Word is neither dirty nor moldy. But it is built layer upon layer like an onion. And seeing these layers (and separating them) is rewarding.

Take the familiar story of the good Samaritan in Luke 10:30-37. There is the story itself, which everybody knows. Many cities have a Good Samaritan Hospital. Good Sam Clubs get their name here. From the story we learn to DO GOOD.

Either John 4:9 or our Sunday school teacher tells us that Jews and Samaritans were enemies. They didn't even speak. The lesson becomes, DO GOOD TO YOUR ENEMIES, as interpreted by Jesus in 36 and 37.

Down another layer, a type of Christ emerges (types and shadows are discussed on p.57). A first aid instructor can use the passage to demonstrate good first aid techniques. The Samaritan (1) acted promptly, (2) acted out of compassion, (3) was prepared, (4) did the best thing available in his day, and (5) didn't leave the victim until the job was done.

A preacher might peel off still another layer and use the story as an example of religious hypocrisy on the part of the two who passed by.

Not only must the Bible speak to people with a wide range of backgrounds, it must also speak to people in other generations than ours. The Bible was written for people throughout history. The layers reflect this.

The book of Joel is a good example. To be from God, a prophet had to be 100 percent correct. That's a tough act to put together if you are not from God. Nearly every Old Testament prophet condemned Israel for her faults—really chewed the Jews out. And yet the Jews very carefully preserved these writings that bad-mouthed them. Why? Because the writers had proved themselves 100 percent right. They spoke for God.

Onion layers, then, may represent more than just applications or interpretations. They may picture different times. The prophet may prove himself—establish his credentials—when his prophecies come true not long after he makes them. They may be fulfilled again in a later generation. And many, which have been fulfilled several times already, may be fulfilled again during the end times, or last days.

In the case of Joel, he begins by describing a locust plague. It happened. His reputation was established (Amos may have mentioned that very plague in Amos 4:9).

The locusts were literal. But apparently Joel was also speaking figuratively of invading armies. Historians believe the four kinds of locusts in Joel 1:4 represent four different empires that invaded Israel:

• Assyria-Babylon, which carried Israel into exile

- Medo-Persia, which let Israel go home but kept the people under a heavy yoke
- Greece-Macedonia, which inflicted inhuman horrors on the Jews, especially before the Maccabbean revolt
- Rome, which completely wiped out the Jews as a nation

Many scholars believe that Joel is speaking to our generation also, for the promises in chapter 2—especially verses 19 through 26—seem to be coming true right now.

And finally, Joel speaks over and over of the end times, the great Day of the Lord. Does this spell out our near future?

Joel gets deeper and deeper, the more you get into history and prophecy. And yet the anguish of the locust plague remains to be appreciated for itself.

Literal or Figurative?

"Horseplay." "Striking a Happy Medium." "Passing the Buck." The pictures are silly because when we say those words we don't mean them literally.

"Literally" means "right down to the letter." Exactly what the words say. "Figurative" means "a figure or picture," a symbol of something else. In Joel, the locusts were literal but symbolized future armies. To the Jews of Jesus' day, a dog was a Roman soldier. But it is also a furry animal that goes, "Woof". "Animal" is the literal meaning, "soldier" the figurative.

As a rule of thumb, try to take the Bible's words literally whenever you can. In fact, a passage may often be taken both ways at once, providing a variety of meanings in one sentence. For instance: in Psalm 22, most of the experiences described never actually happened to the psalmist, David. But they did happen to the Messiah a thousand years later. The psalm mentions sensations that crucifixion would produce. In verse 16, "dogs" probably means Roman soldiers. But again, they might be actual dogs, slinky scavengers.

Some passages you must take figuratively. In Genesis chapter 49, Jacob blesses each of his children. In verse 14 he calls Issachar an ass, and in verse 21 Naphtali is a female deer that bears comely fawns. His sons, of course, were normal human beings. So you start seeking figurative meanings.

Sometimes you'll really have to dig. A Syrian woman (not a Jew) begs Jesus to drive a demon out of her daughter (Matthew 15:22-28). She seems to be talking nonsense. But Jesus praises her and grants her wish. What did she say?

First, Jesus quotes the Old Testament to explain why He was ignoring her (v. 24). The "lost sheep" are Jews, and He gets that from many Old Testament passages— Jeremiah 10, 23, and 25; Ezekiel 34; Micah 5:4; Zechariah 10:3—Jesus is here to help the Jews.

When she blocks His path, He speaks to her figuratively. Children = children of Israel = Jews (Exodus 1:7). Bread = Jesus and His works (John 6:35). Dogs are non-Jews, remember? And that includes the Syrian woman. "Why," Jesus is saying, "should I give you something meant for Jews?"

This sharp lady picks up the figure immediately. And she bounces it right back to Him (v. 27). "Yea, Lord. I, a non-Jew, am content with any little bit of mercy You are willing to let fall. I don't ask for a full blessing—just this one request" (author's paraphrase).

She calls Him Lord and Master. She is confident that the least gesture from Him is enough to exorcise her daughter's demon. She has the spiritual insight to understand His figurative speech and give it back to Him (something His own disciples usually missed, as in John 16:29). What a fantastic faith that lady has!

Is the Jonah story figurative or literal? Jesus treated it as though it actually happened. He took the Scriptures literally.

Even when it seems a passage could only be figurative, literal flowers bloom unexpectedly. Few theologians in the 1700s believed the Jews would really come home to the Holy Land. Cotton Mather did. He believed Exodus 19:4 (with Isaiah 40:31) would be enacted literally. In fact, he said, the Jews one day would possess wings like eagles and fly home. Today Jews are pouring into the Holy Land on El Al, TWA, and other airlines. TWA, the second largest carrier into Lod, is based in the United States—and the United States emblem is the eagle.

Perspective

You don't just look at something. You look at it *from* somewhere. Where you are when you look at the something might be physical. For instance, a horse looks different from different angles:

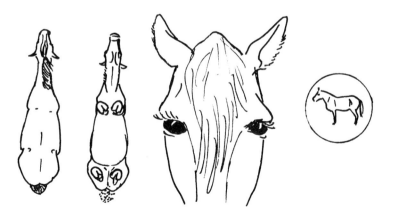

Your position provides a perspective. Your attitude does, too. Attitude is especially important if you have a strong opinion about the something you are looking at. Again, that horse—which is owned by a riding stable, let's say—looks different to different people because of their different attitudes:

The owner of an Arabian

The owner of the stable

The Bible writers all had a perspective—they wrote from a viewpoint. It could even have been physical. When John described his Revelation visions he was apparently in a place where he could see heaven (Revelation 4:2, 6:9, etc.) and earth (e.g., 6:12, 15) at the same time. He tells us what was happening in both places.

Novice rider

An experienced rider who wants to GO

Paul explains how he handled perspectives in 1 Corinthians 9:19-23. He first put himself in the other person's shoes. Once there, he started from one perspective and brought his listener around to another.

Finally there is your own perspective—the topmost, overall viewpoint from which you look at the Word. Theologian Nels Ferré calls it superspective—the center of focus of all your spiritual seeing. It is the very heart, the core of the onion you are peeling. The core of the onion shapes and supports all those outer layers—crooked center, crooked onion. Your superspective will govern how much you understand the mind of God in His Scriptures.

What is your overall, ultimate perspective? What are you looking for at the very heart of God's Word? Your answer, after you've thought about it, might be a long philosophical statement. It may be, very simply, "Jesus." Consider carefully, for your superspective will affect your understanding of Scripture very much.

Pitfalls

Even before Jesus ascended into heaven He was being misunderstood (for instance, John 21:22-23). Sooner or later, you and I will get something wrong. It's unavoidable, but that's no excuse for a cop-out. Base your opinions firmly in Scripture and be ready to change them only when your growing understanding of Scripture tells you they need changing. We make mistakes, but the Scripture does not.

Another pitfall is "taking a passage out of context." Context is the writing that comes before the passage and follows after—the whole picture of which your passage is part.

To be silly for a moment, let me show you that God is in favor of highway billboards and those old Burma Shave signs:

> "And the Lord answered me:
> 'Write the vision;
> make it plain upon tablets,
> so he may run who reads it'"
> (Habakkuk 2:2, RSV).*

My proof is pretty good, huh? Not when you read the verses that come before and after. God wasn't instructing Habakkuk in billboard advertising at all.

Certain cults are experts at taking passages out of their contexts. They will take two well-known lines from the Bible and connect those two passages with their own word. Suddenly the meaning comes out backwards to what the whole context tells you.

God expects us to be like the Bereans in Acts 17:11. We are to examine every claim and form every opinion by searching the Scriptures. He wouldn't expect it of us if He didn't know we can do it.

So step out boldly, knowing that you are in His perfect will!

*Revised Standard Version.

6

REFLECTIONS IN THE LIVING WATER

"With joy shall ye draw water out of the wells of salvation" (Isaiah 12:3).

"They [Israel] have forsaken Me [the Lord], the fountain of living waters" (Jeremiah 2:13, NASB).

"In that day . . . living waters will flow out of Jerusalem" (Zechariah 14:8, NASB).

"For the Lamb . . . will guide them to springs of living water" (Revelation 7:17, RSV). "If any man is thirsty, let him come to Me and drink. He who believes in Me, as the Scripture said, 'From his innermost being shall flow rivers of living water'" (Jesus in John 7:37-38, NASB).

Each of these references reflects upon the others.

Each helps you understand the others better.

Each points to Jesus, at least ultimately. And by saying the words "living water," Jesus identifies the passages with Himself—He points us to the Old Testament, which points right back to the New.

Many themes and truths weave through the Bible from book to book, reflecting one upon another. Now how do you find these reflections?

The Use of Cross-references

Cross-references help you tie together related thoughts and similar passages. A reference edition of the Bible will have one or more of these references as a note in the John 7 passage, for instance. A concordance provides you with ample cross-references. Look up key words of the phrase in question (in our example here, "water," especially "living water").

But Jesus Himself is the primary, direct source. F'rinstance: sometimes He quotes an Old Testament phrase directly, as in Mark 7:6-8. There He quotes Isaiah and applies the passage to the people listening to Him. Other times He simply reflects an Old Testament passage: "As it was in the days of Noah. . . ." "As Jonah was three days in. . . ." "As Moses lifted up the serpent in the wilderness. . . ." Stop when He says those things. Go back and look them up.

Let's take this serpent business a moment. What could Moses' brass snake have to do with Jesus? Since He made the reflection, we check it out. A reference edition will tell you where the story is found in the Old Testament. Or look up "serpent" in a concordance. There are many serpent references, but only two that mention Moses in the same breath—John 3:14 and Numbers 21:4-9.

Yeah, but Numbers 21:4-9 doesn't make sense! Well, think figuratively.

Snakebite was fatal. Sin is fatal.

Looking saved. Faith saves.

The cure doesn't make sense. But then, says Paul, neither does the gospel to the unsaved (1 Corinthians 1:18).

The agent of cure was raised on a pole, prominently, for all to look upon. Nor did one perform a work. The looking saved. Salvation is not by works (Ephesians 2:8-9).

If your Bible study group is getting solidly into the Word, it starts to get exciting here. Everyone finds more ways in which the brass serpent reflects the gospel. The cure was complete—no partials, no cripples. The matter was urgent. Nobody could do it for you. You had to make your own commitment, your own looking. But another could help you along to a point where you could see the pole. It was available to all. This sort of brainstorming is tough at first, because you have no background in Scripture yet. But it will get easier and easier and more rewarding.

Sometimes Jesus didn't have the time or inclination to spell out His references. On the cross He cried out, "My God, My God, why hast thou forsaken me?" (Matthew 27:46). Your reference edition sends you, in a footnote, to Psalm 22:1. Or maybe you remember seeing it. Or, since Jesus said that, you look up a key word in a concordance ("forsaken," perhaps).

Psalm 22 was written one thousand years before the Romans made use of crucifixion. Such never happened to David at all. How many of the events of Psalm 22 happened at Jesus' death? Could He have "fixed" them if He wished to set Himself up as a phony Messiah? Remember that dogs can be Roman soldiers, too. There's material for half an hour of serious discussion right there.

Typical Typical

A type, or shadow, is a picture of a reality. It is a hint or promise of something else. The book of Hebrews, for instance, is loaded with types—Melchizedek, Abraham, the tabernacle—and most are explained right there.

In the serpent passage above, the brass serpent was typical of Christ.

A type of Christ might be a single word. In 1 Corinthians 10:1-5, Paul explains how "the Rock" is typical of Christ. When you come to a passage of that sort, stop reading and take some time to look up "rock" passages (or whatever the subject is) in a concordance. If "the Rock" is a type of Christ, try substituting the name Jesus Christ for rock.

John did the same thing with "Word" in his gospel, John 1:1-2. Read Psalm 119, thinking of Jesus as you read "word."

As you become more accustomed to this kind of thing, it will get easier and easier. And the easier it gets, the more you will see. You will soon find it fruitful to be thinking the way the Jews thought.

Jesus called Himself the Good Shepherd in John 10:11. How picturesque! Now artists will have something nice to draw—Jesus being a shepherd—maybe a halo, and a lamb around His shoulders. But to the Jews, His statement was a theological blockbuster. He wasn't being cute. He was setting Himself up as the Messiah.

Spotting something like this doesn't happen the first time you read through the Bible. But later, as you are growing in Scripture, you'll feel comfortable looking things up in a concordance. And you'll remember a lot of what you've seen somewhere before.

In this case, a concordance or topical Bible will have references to the "good shepherd." You'll find Psalm 23 (which you already knew), Isaiah 40:11, Ezekiel 34, Hebrews 13:20, and many others. All tie in the shepherd with God's Messiah. These are what Jesus pointed to with that single, simple statement.

Now wait! Why all this business about types? Why not just say, "Jesus is such and so"?

Remember that the Scriptures must speak to people in every culture in every age. With types, cross-references, and symbolism of various sorts, the Bible can say many different things in just one passage. The passage can speak to different backgrounds in different eras. It is a universal picture everyone can see and understand, each according to his personal abilities. God uses this method to feed us all we are ready for, regardless of the age or culture to which we are born.

God's mind is far too complex for us to understand from just one book of flat statements. Peeling the onion helps us see Him just a bit better.

7

HELP FOR THE SYMBOL-MINDED

Symbols. The federal government peppers them all over our national parks. Wordless picture-signs label everything from rest rooms to snowmobile routes. A major broadcasting company spends hundreds of thousands of dollars on a two-color logo that flashes for only a moment across your TV screen. Topographic maps, the Christmas season, railroad timetables, this written page—where would we be without symbols?

Types are actually symbols. So are parables, in a way. We already mentioned dogs as being symbols for Roman soldiers. The fig tree and myrtle tree have always been symbols for Israel. So Zechariah (1:10) and Jesus (Matthew 24:32) used them.

Some symbols are explained right in the Scripture. The rainbow in Genesis is an example (9:12-18).

But understanding of many symbols has developed through the centuries as men's knowledge of the Word has grown. Knowing them will help you understand deeper meanings.

Below is a starter's list. Eventually, you may want to purchase a book just on symbols in Scripture. Don't memorize. Think and reason—they fall into line if you think about them. Then they are a part of you, not something to be forgotten. "Oh, yeah! I see that now!"

- gold: divine glory; faith
- silver: redemptive work of Christ (thirty pieces)
- blue: Christ's heavenly character (sky)
- purple: Christ's royal character, kingly nature
- scarlet: Christ's redeeming character (blood)
- linen: Christ's sinless, spotless character
                     (linen is naturally white)
- oil: the Holy Spirit ("anoint" comes from a
                     word for oil)
- spices: the fragrance of Christ, especially
                     before God
- raven: Satan, darkness
- dove: Holy Spirit; peace with God; promise
- brass: Christ's death (brazen or bronze, too)
- goat hair: practical; serviceable; simple
- ram's skin: devotedness in the priestly office
- gems: preciousness of God to His people
- acacia: (also called shittim or gopher wood)
                     permanence—resisting corruption, as
                     acacia is exceedingly durable

Jesus was famous for curing the sick, the handicapped, and—on occasion—the dead. Often He would preach a message directly related to a miracle of healing, as in John 11:25, 44. Thus, diseases and such have come to symbolize spiritual afflictions.

- death: our natural state in sin
- leprosy: defilement and loneliness of sin
- palsy: enfeeblement, helplessness of sin
- blindness: darkness and ignorance of sin
- deafness: inability to hear God because of
                     the barrier of sin
- dumbness: inability to speak spiritual truth
- fever: restlessness and contagion of sin
- crippling: impotence apart from God

Numerology and astrology are centuries older than Scripture. But the Word forbids us to use them. Applying a nonscriptural meaning to a scriptural symbol is a no-no. However, certain numbers seem to symbolize certain things in Scripture. For instance:

- 1   unity
- 2   full measure
- 3   divine (Trinity = 3 persons)
- 4   earth (4 corners, 4 winds, 4 directions)
- 5   human responsibility
- 6   incomplete; fallen short
- 7   complete; the sum of divine (3) and earth (4); total
- 10   2 (full measure) times 5 (human responsiblity) = the number of law
- 12   God's governmental number for earth (e.g. Matthew 19:28, Revelation 4:4 where 2x12=24; 2=full measure)
- 40   2x4x5=full measure of man's responsibility on earth; thus, a time of testing, probation, judgment; also, a generation.

Three times any number means special emphasis. The number of the Antichrist is revealed as 666; this is an extreme emphasis on the incompleteness, or nondivinity of the Antichrist—the ultimate fall-short.

8

HELP! HELP!

Guess you noticed by now—as you begin digging deeper into the Word, looking at types and shadows, finding cross-references—a concordance starts getting pretty handy. There are a number of useful study helps. As you become more comfortable in the Word, you will actually enjoy digging things out with them.

Here are some study helps you will want to investigate before too long.

Commentary

A commentary makes comments. It's that simple. A paraphrase is a commentary of sorts. So are some Bible study courses. Not every commentary, though, is a good one. Helpful commentaries do these things:

- provide tables to make confusing parts easier to see: tables of the kings of Israel, time lines, tables of prophets and their eras, and so forth
- provide explanations for difficult passages—more than one explanation, if there are strong differences of opinion
- relate archaeology to Scripture
- tie related Scriptures together

Avoid any commentary that tries to push a particular sectarian viewpoint and any commentary that does not respect the Bible (some, for instance, might try to explain away uncomfortable things like Jonah and the whale). Ask yourself and others who know, "Does this commentary honor Jesus and the Word?"

Concordance

This is your most useful study aid. The classic, complete concordances are based on King James. However, the *New American Standard Bible,* Revised Version, and Revised Standard Version work fairly well with them. New concordances to the modern translations will get better and better.

Cruden's is a popular beginner's concordance. It is straight alphabetical. Strong's and Young's are more sophisticated. They list words by alphabet and also by the original Greek and Hebrew words. They are more detailed but harder to use.

Here's a for-instance:

In Cruden's, the word "spin" is listed thus:

SPIN

Ex. 35:25 wise-hearted, did *s.*

Mat. 6:28 neither *s. Luke* 12:27

The English word *spin* occurs in Exodus and in Matthew in the phrases abbreviated above. The Matthew quotation occurs in the same way in Luke. The other words included in the phrase are to tickle your memory. As you become familiar with the Word, "neither spin" will remind you of the whole quotation, "Consider the lilies of the field. . . ."

In Young's *Analytical:*

SPIN, to—

1. To spin **טָוָה** *tavah*

Exod 35.25 women that were wise hearted did spin
35.26 stirred them up in wisdom spun goats'

2. To spin **νήθω** *nēthō*
   Matt 6.28 the lilies...toil not, neither do they spin
   Luke 12.27 the lilies...toil not, they spin not
It's all a matter of how much detail you want to wade through.

Concordances are used backwards and forwards. You may want to find a passage, but you only remember snatches of it. "Something about lilies toiling—uh—" Look up one or more of the words you remember, and the other words of the passage will help you find the reference numbers.

To work a concordance the other way, you may wish to find out what the Bible says about a word. Perhaps you are researching Jesus' statement, "I am the bread of life." All the relevant words are under "bread."

Topical Bible

But maybe you want to find out about something, and that something isn't mentioned by name. For instance, "insects." There are no insects in the concordance under "i." A topical Bible would have it.

A topical Bible lists things by subject. "Trees" would include all the trees, not just the appearance of the word "tree."

Bible Dictionary

An exhaustive Bible dictionary runs four volumes, three volumes more than the Bible itself. A one-volume dictionary is plenty for most folks. Most popular dictionaries list nouns—people, places, and things. They are excellent for background information. They discuss tools, jewelry, et cetera; give brief biographies; and describe geography.

Atlas

Think of an atlas and you think of a huge, heavy book of maps, maps, maps. But most Bible atlases are largely text.

Like a geography book, they have photos and drawings of the country, with maps here and there. Most of the information in the text is also in good dictionaries and commentaries.

The face of the Holy Land has changed much in four thoqsand years. Place name change, cities and regions disappear as names. The climate and vegetation have changed somewhat. Good maps help these changes make sense. They help the travels of Jesus and Paul make sense and come alive.

Modern maps of the Holy Land are interesting. But unless they also give traditional scripture names, they are of no value in Bible study.

Greek and Hebrew Lexicons

Lexicon is a fancy word for "foreign language dictionary." In it you will find the Greek or Hebrew words written in Greek or Hebrew letters. The rest of the entry is like a dictionary—definition and where located. A lexicon, with a Greek or Hebrew text, is very important for advanced Bible scholars. Most laymen live their whole lives very comfortably with them.

If you are adventurous and wish to try New Testament Greek, you can do it several ways. If there is a Bible college nearby, sign up for Greek as a night course. There are also excellent correspondence courses in Greek, with taped lectures, texts, and personal help.

For more casual use of Greek, you can buy a Greek text (either the old Stephens 1550 or the new Westcott-Hort). An interlinear text will have English translation of the Greek words between the lines in the Greek text. Usually the text also features the King James Version or a straight English translation as a parallel column down the side. Chapter and verse numbers help you know where you are.

If you choose to study Greek on your own, you must

first memorize the Greek alphabet. Fraternity initiates must be able to strike a match and recite the Greek alphabet three times before they may blow out the match. There are few frat rats with charred fingers. If a lowly pledge can learn it, so can you.

Even if you have no desire to actually learn Greek, being familiar with it makes your study richer. For Greek is a very subtle, very expressive language. And there are meanings in the Greek that are lost in even the best English versions.

For example: John 21:15-17 is a puzzling dialogue between Peter and the risen Jesus. It seems Peter is getting upset at the repetitious questions. The word translated "love" here is actually two different words in Greek. *Phileo* φιλέω is a brotherly affection (Philadelphia = brotherly love). You-love-me-and-I'll-love-you. *Agape* ἀγάπη, however, is a far loftier love. It is the very highest level of love attainable—God's love that loves without being loved in return, if need be.

In verse 15 of the John 21 passage, Jesus uses *agape*. Peter is impulsive but honest. He cannot attain to that high level. The best he can honestly reply with is *phileo*. "Yes, Lord, I *phileo* you."

In verse 16, again Jesus uses *agape*. Again, Peter is stuck with his *phileo*.

In verse 17, Jesus takes a big, big step down. "Peter, do you *phileo* me?" "You know everything, Lord. It's *phileo*." Peter was terribly disappointed and upset, not with Jesus but with himself. He had let his Lord down. Jesus was forced into second best.

PS. The story has a happy ending. Peter apparently mastered *agape*. Because in 1 Peter 1:22 (his letter to the church), he writes, "Having purified your souls with *phileo*, *agape* one another from the heart" (author's paraphrase).

Other Aids

Some Bibles have study aids built right in. The *Thompson Chain Reference Bible* uses a unique system of accumulating references to specific topics. The *Scofield Reference Bible* is a sort of commentary and Bible combined. The *Second Coming Bible* is in itself a study in prophecy. The *Amplified Bible* not only translates the Greek and Hebrew but puts in parentheses additional words into which the Greek might be translated. It gives you a feel for the subtle nuances of the original language. The *Ryrie Study Bible* provides a harmony of the gospels, a topical index, timeline charts, a synopsis of Bible teaching (Scripture, God, angels, salvation, etc.), and a suggested schedule for reading through the Bible in a year.

Remember, though, that no study aid or fancy version will do you any good if you are not comfortable using it. Let your own skills and preferences choose the aids you own.

9

NOW THAT YOU'VE GOT IT ...

...What are you going to do with it?

Here is everyone telling you to get into Bible study, but no one has said why.

"What's in it for me?"

The Mind of God

People sometimes say they wish they could meet So-and-So, the greatest intellectual of his day (whoever he is and whatever the day). Here is your chance to meet the greatest intellectual and creative force in all history—God Himself. Simply to know something of the mind of God is one of the greatest blessings you will ever have.

The Mind of Christ

Now how can you please the Master of your life if you don't know anything about Him?

Jesus is the Word (John 1:1).

The Scriptures are the Word (Psalm 119).

In a very real sense, Jesus and Scripture are one—one explains the other, the other fulfills the one. To explore Scripture is to explore the mind of Christ. To know the Christ is to know the most beautiful and compassionate Person who ever lived as a man. You can admire the complexity of His wisdom and the simplicity of His truth, all at once.

Duty

God is the giver of all good gifts. But He also has great expectations for us. We have certain privileges and responsibilities as Christians. They are all explained in the Bible. What is heaven like? The Bible only hints. What is hell like? A few hints are plenty. Most important, since we have been assigned to heaven, and hell has been denied us, we have certain duties. They are not payment for services rendered by God. They are not dues, or fire insurance. God would have us perform our duties as Christians because we love Him. And we love Him because He first loved us. Our duties are not payment of a bill owed God, but debts of love we can never repay—but it is most gratifying to try.

God's expectations for us are explained in Scripture in examples, outright statements, and broad principles. Some are not commands. That makes them all the more important to be performed.

Purpose

A sense of purpose is a basic need. We must have a value, a reason for breathing. The Christian's purpose is to do the will of God—to praise Him, to bear fruit for glory. The deeper you get into the Word, the more clearly you see God's purpose. And therefore the better you can see your own purpose. The more you see, then, the better you can serve.

Now this is all theory. The bottom line is: Exactly how do I put Bible knowledge into practical use? We live from day to day, not from theory to theory.

Personal Guidance

God made us. That makes the Bible the manufacturer's handbook. Even if you are not a Christian, scriptural principles afford the richest and most hassle-free life. As Christians, we have the added desire to live God's way because we belong to Him.

The Bible offers instruction by three methods:

Direct rules. Certain points are spelled out plainly. In 2 Corinthians 6:14, Paul warns against linking up with unbelievers. The good, solid rule can be applied to a number of situations.

Example. The good Samaritan provides a good example, Ananias and his wife in Acts 5 provide quite another. Ezra called himself a ready scribe (Ezra 7:6), so we can take pen in hand, following his example. We might write a letter to a friend who needs one. The friend may need Jesus. If he has Jesus, he may need encouragement. We may borrow someone else's pen by giving a book or tract away.

Precepts. Certain suggestions are in the form of very general statements. Romans 14:23 says that whatever does not proceed from faith is sin. James 4:17 says that whoever knows what is right and fails to do it, for him it is sin. God gives you the basic lump and invites you to help Him form the final sculpture of your life. And that is the ultimate in creativity!

Cross-fertilization

The Christian has three responsibilities—to God, to others, and to himself, and they are all interlinked.

The people you talk to are either saved or unsaved. The unsaved need sound, God-centered answers, not a lame "You just have to take it on faith, that's all."

The saved will either be weaker or stronger than you. The strong need fellowship. The weak need support and uplifting. Again this must come from your own solid foundation. "Well, I think" is no help. "The Bible says right here" surely is.

The Bible-based Christian is productive. He is a rich source of seed for God to sow among unbelievers. He is a rich source of nutrients and water for fellow believers. He is fruitful in the best sense of the word.

One of the best ways to build each other up is regular home Bible study. This is not the daily study you are doing on your own. Rather it is Christians gathering on a regular (usually weekly) basis for group study.

How many? Six is a good number. Ten is a mite unwieldy. It is nice but not essential that most members be at about the same level of spiritual maturity. One or two members should be well-versed in the Scripture. Here's why. Questions get answered promptly and pertinent verses found more quickly. While the new Christian doesn't know something is there, the advanced student at least vaguely remembers something about it.

But there is also a strong disadvantage. Be aware of it in order to avoid it. The more mature may find himself sort of taking over, perhaps without meaning or wanting to. And the less mature will start leaning on him instead of doing the work themselves.

Conduct the study in one place or float from home to home. X may have small children who should be in bed at 7:30. So X might prefer it to be held in his home weekly. In that case, W, Y, and Z take turns bringing the snacks.

And there will be goodies. Christians never seem to get together without food and drink somehow. Snacks and good conversation after the study enhance fellowship.

First, select a leader. This is not necessarily the most mature person. In fact, he probably shouldn't be. If the study floats from place to place, the host may simply take over. If the study meets in one place, leadership might rotate. The leader's job is to keep the study moving. He does *not* monopolize the evening. He guards against argon.

"Argon?" Argon is a Greek word borrowed by scientists to name an inert element. It means something absolutely useless. A sunsuit for an Eskimo. Still another bump on a log. Drivel. No redeeming value. Zilch. And argon can sink a Bible study quicker than you can say, "Methuselah enthused over Ma's loose sealers."

When conversation leaves the subject at hand, the leader (or whoever notices what has happened) yells, "Argon! Argon!" and all conversation ceases. Back to work.

What to study?

Guided study. There are study guides for advanced students and guides for beginners. You can obtain them from a local Bible bookstore or from any of several correspondence instruction institutions. Avoid any study guide that points to a particular sect or denomination. Some claim that guided study is the only way for beginners. Discuss and decide as a group.

Multi-version study. Each member brings a different version or paraphrase. The group reads the given passage in the various versions and discusses cross-references, footnotes, and comments each may have.

Book or author. The group may wish to study one particular author or one special book. It is wisest, if your group is new in the Word, to explore the New Testament first. Read a passage. Consider the points (types, symbolism, etc.) this book recommends for individual study. Scout out the cross-references, hash out ideas. When ideas start to dry up, move on. You will find yourselves covering three chapters one evening and three verses the next time. The Spirit will lead. Ask Him!

Topic. More advanced students often gain much from choosing a topic. Everyone finds what he can on it (how about: the wife's duties; child-raising; successful parents in Scripture; love in the Old Testament). Divide your topic into sub-topics for several weeks' work. Child-raising, for instance, might be divided into successful parenthood (Hannah with Samuel), parental failure (Eli with his sons;

Solomon's brood), and how not to do it (Rebekah with Esau and Jacob).

Question-discussion. Everyone brings one question to the study. It may come from his studies during the week. It may be unrelated to anyone else's. It can be very basic or very brainy. Any sincere question is a good one. Then everyone chips in to build an answer, considering as many ramifications as possible. Some for-instances: What did Jesus mean in Matthew 12:43-45? Why didn't some Jews want Esther to be in the canon? What were the differences between Pharisees and Sadduccees? What did David *really* look like?

The ultimate goal of any group study is not to straighten the world out, nor to win a point, nor to prove how smart —or dumb—someone is. The purpose is to build up every member so that he can serve God better where he is.

Moving Right Along

It seems logical to start at the beginning—Genesis. But you will find, probably, that your best beginning is Matthew. The New Testament reveals Jesus outright. The Old Testament is Jesus concealed. The New Testament is shorter. It is God's special message to believers in Christ.

Some passages are a whole lot heavier than others. Some will mean more to you than to someone else and vice versa. In fact, in places you'll find yourself bogging down completely. That's when Satan will be right there at your ear with a discouraging word or two. Don't you listen to him. You will be ready for that difficult passage next time around. Skim over it and go on. Start fresh a chapter or two ahead. Start the next book and come back to this difficult passage later. But keep reading.

The Last Page

This book has a last page.
The Bible does not.

Genesis intertwines with Revelation to weave a tapestry of profound complexity.

God's wisdom extends so far beyond our ability to absorb it that we can study His Word for a lifetime and never run out of new things to see.

So we wrestle with questions that have no answers. We find answers we never dreamed existed. And we wait patiently for His return.

> For now we see in a mirror
> dimly, but then face to face.
> Now I know in part; then I shall
> understand fully, even as I have
> been fully understood. So faith,
> hope, love abide, these three;
> but the greatest of these is
>   love

(1 Corinthians 13:12-13, RSV).

Appendix A
BACKGROUND ON THE BIBLE'S BOOKS

It is helpful to know some background data as you read the books of the Bible. In fact, it's a necessity to know, for instance, why Philemon (a one-pager between Titus and Hebrews, New Testament) was written if you are really to appreciate it.

Here then are some data to help you enjoy reading the Bible more. In some cases Bible scholars vary widely in opinion as to dates. Conservative dates are quoted here. And even if the year fluctuates a bit, the sequence of events is the same and their importance undiminished. And if someone says, "But that old date can't be defended," you may reply with confidence, "You bet your sweet bookmark it can!"

Given are:
- the source of the book's name
- the approximate date
- the author and/or authority
- a brief historical perspective
- in some cases, things to watch for.

THE PENTATEUCH

The first five books of the Old Testament, Genesis through Deuteronomy, are the Pentateuch (*pent* = five, *teuch* = book, or volume). This is the segment Jesus called "the Law" in Matthew 22:40. The Law has significance for both the Jewish and Christian faiths.

And both Jewish and Christian traditions claim Moses as the author, which would date the Pentateuch around 1500 B.C. There has never been a serious question about their authenticity and authority.

GENESIS

(See "Pentateuch.") Genesis means origins, a Greek rendition of the opening words in the original Hebrew, "in the beginning." Genesis covers the history of the Jews from the raw beginning through Abraham (about 2000 B.C. to Joseph in Egypt (1800-1700 B.C.).

Abraham's hometown Ur is well documented archaeologically. It was a center of civilization in his day and leaving Ur behind was like swapping New York City nightlife for a shanty in Idaho. Abraham's route was the "Fertile Crescent" you read about in geography class—the loop up the Tigris-Euphrates valley and down into the Holy Land.

Look for lots of types and pictures here, all pointing to Christ and His sacrifice. This is the foundation of the Messianic proof and promise.

EXODUS

(See "Pentateuch.") Exodus—from Greek meaning "the way out," or "exit"—refers to the Jews' emigration from Egypt. After a sojourn of about four hundred thirty years, they left Egypt about 1500 B.C. (some authorities suggest 1300 B.C.). The Hebrews' status had deteriorated from that of "honored guests" to slaves. They had gone to Egypt to escape a famine long since past and had become so comfortable they stayed. Now God wanted them in the land they had been given, and He would raise up Moses to lead them home.

Who was Pharaoh? Most likely: If Thuthmes III was the great oppressor of the Hebrews, then his successor, Amenhotep II would be the Pharaoh of the Exodus; if Ramses II the oppressor, then his successor, Meneptah. Egypt's Egyptian population at that time was probably around seven million.

The Hebrews here are a brilliant picture of the Christian. God saves us out of the death-dealing world into hope and promise. Still we grumble and long for the old worldly ways now and then, forgetting the bitterness that came with the indulgences of the past.

LEVITICUS

(See "Pentateuch.") The name comes from the Levites, the priestly tribe descended from Levi. To them were given the precise rules of worship, cleaning, and care of the Tabernacle and its accoutrements.

The date is somewhere around 1450 B.C. probably. The Hebrews had been delivered out of slavery in Egypt. Now, in Sinai, they were being organized for worship and travel. When John the Baptist said of Jesus in John 1:29, "Behold the Lamb of God who takes away the sin of the world," he was referring to this book.

NUMBERS

(See "Pentateuch.") The title refers to two censuses of the itinerant Hebrews. They were still in Sinai and because of a lack of faith would remain in Sinai until the last of the old generation (except Caleb and Joshua) died. The children would inherit the promised land. A map will be very helpful to you as you read. Trace the routes and boundaries as you go, else all those names will be meaningless. The date is probably around 1450 B.C.

DEUTERONOMY

(See "Pentateuch.") Deutero- refers to the "second" or the "repeated" law. Leviticus gave the priests their rules. This time the laws were all recited for the common people The date is probably still around 1400 B.C. The Hebrews were now poised on the brink, about to move in and take over their promised land. After forty years only Joshua, Caleb, and Moses were left of the old guard. These were

Moses' final messages to his people. From here they would go on without him.

As you read the blessings and curses, relate them to the Jews' history, including recent history, as you know it.

THE HISTORICAL BOOKS

The Pentateuch is in part historical. The books of Joshua through Esther are primarily historical. This segment of the Old Testament covers the time from when the Israelites entered Canaan, their promised land, until their return from Babylonian captivity—that is, from around 1400 to 445 B.C.

Remember as you read that this Jewish history was concurrent with the ancient history you studied in school. The Assyria, the Babylon, the Egypt, the Persia of the Bible are the nations you have read about.

JOSHUA

Joshua himself may well have written this book bearing his name, somewhere between 1400 and 1250 B.C. The names Joshua and Jesus are nearly synonymous.

The Hebrews had been led by Moses out of slavery in Egypt. After forty years of wandering and purification in the Wilderness of Sinai, they were ready to march across Jordan and commence the conquest of Canaan under the leadership of Joshua. Much richer and more productive than the semi-arid Holy Land we think of today, Canaan really did seem like a farmer's paradise. This book is the story of that conquest.

Watch for many lessons about faith—and lack of it— here. The Rahab in chapters 2 and 6 is the same Rahab listed in Jesus' genealogy (Matthew 1:5).

JUDGES

Judges here were not magistrates. They were leaders from various tribes who rose to an occasion, delivered

their people from some extremity, and then usually
remained in leadership for some time thereafter.

The author is unknown, the dates probably between
1400 and 1100 B.C., give or take some. Joshua had died.
The Hebrews were in their promised land, but there was
no central government, no head over all the tribes. Note
that when one judge needed an army, he had to make up
one piecemeal from various tribes. Judges covers roughly
the first three hundred fifty years of the Jews' life in their
new land.

RUTH

Named for its heroine, this short book took place at
some time during the period of the judges (1400-1100 B.C.)
and is therefore inserted here. The author is not known.

Moab was that land on the bank of the Jordan directly
east of Canaan. This was a foreign country, and Ruth, a
native of Moab, was therefore an alien. Note that she very
clearly gave up the Moabite religion in order to cleave to
Naomi.

That business about redeeming in chapter 4 stemmed
from Moses' message to the Hebrews in Numbers 36 and
Deuteronomy 25:5-10. The land was parceled out to the
Hebrews according to tribe, and they were to keep the
tribal property in the right tribe and family through
inheritance. A dead man's nearest kinsman therefore had
first shot at his property, the second nearest the second
opportunity to obtain it, and so on. Boaz had one other
kinsman nearer Naomi than himself. That fellow had to
forfeit his right before Boaz could take over the dead
Elimelech's inheritance.

1 SAMUEL

This book, named for the priest and judge Samuel, was
once the first half of a single volume now split into 1 and 2
Samuel. The author might have been Ezra. Then again,

perhaps Ezra edited it. Some say Samuel himself wrote it.

The book covers the years 1100 to 1050 B.C. more or less. Israel had been on the skids, with occasional deliverances, for over three hundred years in their new land. Now they wanted a king like other countries had. Samuel was the anointer of kings.

David, born around 1085 B.C., is the most important Messianic figure in the Old Testament. That is, it was from the line of David from the city of David to the throne of David that the Messiah would come. Was David a saint or a heel? As you begin his story in 1 Samuel, reflect on the diversity of his personality—a complex, remarkable man.

2 SAMUEL

(See "1 Samuel" for author, etc.) David probably took the throne of Judah around 1000 B.C. and became king of unified Israel about eight years later. As the book opens, King Saul and his sons were dead and the Philistines had the upper hand—not uncommon at that time. Although Israel had taken over most of Canaan, Jerusalem, controlled by the Jebusites, was a Canaanite island in a Jewish sea. David was born in Bethlehem, less than six miles away, and his first order of business as king was to make Jerusalem Jewish. It wouldn't be easy—the Jebusites were tough and the city well defended.

1 KINGS

The books of 1 and 2 Kings were originally one. Ezra may have edited or even written them. The history here, from David through Solomon to the death of Ahab, spans 965 to 855 B.C., approximately.

David had reigned for a generation (forty years over Judah, thirty-three years over all Israel). Now his throne passed to Solomon. The nation was at peace—David had put down his enemies on every side. Solomon would build the Temple David had considered building. He would also be a prolific writer. In addition to songs and proverbs he would write extensively in the field of natural history (1 Kings 4:32-33), although his secular writings are apparently lost.

Note how Israel's ups and downs dovetail with her spiritual condition.

2 KINGS

See note on 1 Kings regarding authorship. A sad book, this volume sketches history from Ahaziah (c. 855 B.C.) to the demise of Jerusalem in 586 B.C.

The "fall of Jerusalem" was not a once-and-done thing. It occurred in waves over a period of twenty years from 606 to 586 B.C. The date for 2 Kings 24:10 is probably 606, the date for 25:8, 586 B.C. Babylon carried off captives starting with the first stage of destruction, set up puppet governments, and finally wiped out the nation as an entity.

1 CHRONICLES

Again, 1 and 2 Chronicles were originally one book, and Ezra has been cited as either editor or author. But that's conjecture. The time covered is from Adam (4000 B.C. ?) to David (1000 B.C.). The historical comments of 1 and 2 Samuel apply here.

2 CHRONICLES

Here is the other half of Jewish history from Solomon (965 B.C.) to the end of Israel as a nation in 586 B.C. The last paragraph touches upon the fall of Babylon to Persia in 536 B.C. Note that Samuel and Kings deal with the kings of both Judah and the Northern Kingdom, Israel. Chronicles treats only the kings of Judah, the line of David.

EZRA

Ezra, almost certainly the author here, called himself a "ready scribe" (Ezra 7:6). And he was indeed if all the books attributed to him by tradition are really his.

The book of Ezra opens around the year 538 B.C., but Ezra himself does not appear until chapter 7, dated (probably) around 457 B.C. These dates are estimates, understand—you'll find variants elsewhere.

Cyrus of Persia was ruler of the Jews, having taken them as part of the booty of fallen Babylon. Chapter 3 is dated around 536, and 4:24 is then 534 B.C. There is a fourteen year jump as chapter 5 opens. It was now around 520 B.C., and Darius was king as building of the Temple resumed. (Nehemiah, the next Scripture book, fits in right around here.) Ezra entered the scene in chapter 7. Throughout Ezra and Nehemiah the Jews were trickling back to their homeland after seventy years in exile. Their country was wasted, their glory gone. Even the new Temple was a dim shadow of the former glory.

NEHEMIAH

Nehemiah apparently wrote this himself. He ruled around 520-516 B.C. according to some sources, and 444-432 B.C. according to others. As governor, he worked to purify the Jewish line and worship. After the Babylonian destruction, Ezra had commenced clean-up, and Nehemiah was continuing the job. Malachi was a contemporary here (his is the final book of Old Testament prophecy).

ESTHER

Some say Mordecai wrote Esther, others say no. The date is probably 478-473 B.C. Ahasuerus was Xerxes, one of the greatest of Persian kings, who reigned from 485 to 465 B.C. He was the Xerxes of ancient history at the battles of Salamis and Thermopylae.

The story took place in Persia. When that country conquered Babylon, many Jews ended up in Persia as captives. They seem to have adjusted to Persian life very well. Mordecai was well esteemed, and Esther was in the running for queen. Note that, although some Jews were returning to their native land at this time (e.g., Ezra and Nehemiah), other Jews were staying put. Esther apparently was queen after the rebuilding of the Temple at Jerusalem but before the walls were rebuilt.

Some conservative Jews reject Esther from Scripture because, among other things, the Lord's name is nowhere mentioned in the book.

THE POETICAL BOOKS

Much poetry—the Greeks' for example—is based on myth and fancy. The Jews based theirs on solid fact, praise, and worship. In spite of being so practical they still had a rare gift for poetry, magnified by the fact that Hebrew itself is a most poetic language.

Job through Song of Songs compose this segment.

JOB

Job (pronounced Jobe) is borderline between history and poetry and makes a nice connecting link. Tradition dates the story very early—during the days of Abraham— and says Moses had a hand in the writing of it.

It is not too difficult to keep track of who is speaking. When the first verse of a chapter says, "And So-and-so spake," So-and-so is responsible for that whole chapter until someone else speaks.

PSALMS

"Psalms" comes from the Greek word for a kind of song, or ode, and the book is exactly that—a hymnal for worship. The dates of writing stretch from 1000 B.C. or earlier to 580 B.C. or later. David, an accomplished musician, was probably responsible for over half the psalms. "Of," "to," and "for" are all the same Hebrew preposition, so we aren't always sure whether a song was written by, for, or in dedication to someone.

Some aspects of these psalms are lost in our English version. For example, Psalm 119 is divided into twenty-two stanzas in the Hebrew to correspond to the twenty-two letters of the Hebrew alphabet. Each stanza has eight verses, and each of these verses begins with the same letter. The construction is a dandy memory aid for choir singers!

PROVERBS

Proverbs are pithy one-liners, nuggets of wisdom. The first twenty-four chapters are almost certainly by the hand of Solomon, which places them around 900 B.C. The remainder are probably his also, either written by himself or compiled by others from his collection.

ECCLESIASTES

In Greek, *Ecclesiastes* is "preacher." In Hebrew it means especially a leader who assembles a congregation who will hear him preach. The feminine of the Hebrew word suggests wisdom, a deliberate play on words. This book was probably written near the end of Solomon's life, around 930 B.C. Solomon is thought to be the author.

Of the three books attributed to Solomon, Proverbs was assembled throughout his life, Song of Songs reflects a youthful (and lusty) exuberance, and this book reveals the disillusionment and weariness of old age. This man had owned it all and done it all. He wanted desperately a non-material reason for living—a Savior—and he could not find one. Here is a lyric description of human nature.

Compare Solomon here with what we know of David's philosophies. David, a prolific writer, never mentioned any empty feeling. He experienced ethereal highs and abysmal lows, but never did he lose track of his purpose in life—to love and praise God.

SONG OF SOLOMON

Song of Songs, Canticles, Song of Solomon—the content of this book was once considered so delicate that men below the age of thirty were not permitted to read it. The poetic structure in Hebrew is well-nigh perfect. It is actually a song, too, to be performed by a bride voice, a groom voice, and a choir of women's voices. The parts aren't always easy to pick out, and quite probably there was repetition of choruses and stanzas here and there.

Some Christians interpret the book as a picture of the church as Bride and Jesus as her Groom.

If Solomon wrote this early in his reign, the date would be about 965 B.C.

THE PROPHETS

A creditable Messiah does not simply appear out of the woodwork. He must have proofs of his Messiahship. The prophets provide some of Jesus' most convincing credentials. Four to eight centuries before Jesus was born, they foretold minute details of His life and ministry and precise details of His death. The prophetic books are not the only prophecy—David, for instance, made many prophetic points several hundred years before the early prophets— but the prophets' books are gathered here under the authors' names. Remember as you read that the prophets fit into the history of Samuel through Nehemiah.

Isaiah, Jeremiah, Ezekiel, and Daniel are known as the "major prophets"; Hosea through Malachi are the "minor prophets." This has nothing to do with the weightiness of their messages but rather with the weightiness of their books—with small exception, the writings of the "major prophets" are longer.

ISAIAH

With his opening words Isaiah dated himself—the reigns of Uzziah through Hezekiah, about 740-700 B.C. ± . The history of his time is recorded in 2 Kings 14:17 through 2 Kings 20 and in 2 Chronicles 26 through 32 ± .

Look up Assyria in an encyclopedia. Throughout his life Isaiah knew the Assyrian empire as The Enemy and watched it grow as a military threat. The Assyrians enjoyed a fine reputation for cruelty toward the peoples they conquered, so fear of Assyria was not strictly political. Eventually Assyria would destroy Israel utterly and take a big chunk out of Judah. Over one hundred years after Isaiah, Assyria would get her comeuppance from Babylon.

Isaiah was a contemporary of the prophets Jonah, Amos, Hosea, and Micah (his father, Amoz, is not the prophet Amos but another). Isaiah was the most Messianic of the prophets. Tradition says Manasseh sawed him in two—he would have been about eighty-five years old then.

JEREMIAH

Jeremiah means "whom the LORD has appointed."

One hundred years after Isaiah, world power was shifting. The Assyrians were crushed, and Babylon and Egypt now struggled for supremacy. Against Jeremiah's advice the Israelites were courting Egypt as their ally. Egypt lost the power struggle to Babylon at Carchemish in 605 B.C. And Jerusalem was invaded.

Jeremiah's ministry was during the final hour of Jerusalem, as recorded in 2 Kings 24-25 and 2 Chronicles 36. No wonder Jeremiah was "the weeping prophet" as he watched his beloved nation die before his eyes. Tradition says he was taken down to Egypt against his will and there he was stoned. The Egyptian remnant of the Jews was destroyed.

A contemporary of the prophets Zephaniah and Habakkuk at home and Daniel and Ezekiel in exile, Jeremiah was also author of the Lamentations following his prophetic book.

LAMENTATIONS

Lamentations are cries of grief, expressions of extreme sorrow. Jeremiah wrote these elegies to lament the destruction of Jerusalem, around 586 B.C. Each chapter is a separate elegy. Today this poetic dirge is still read on the ninth day of the fourth month in every synagogue, commemorating the fall of Jerusalem.

In chapters 1, 2 and 4, the beginning letters of each verse in the Hebrew are in alphabetical order. Chapter 3 has sixty-six verses, three for each letter, and chapter 5 has a verse for each letter, but they're not alphabetical.

EZEKIEL

Ezekiel means "strength of God."

This book was written about the time of the end of Israel. Babylon was in the process of picking the last of the meat from Judah's bones. Since 606 B.C. she had been carrying Jews captive to Babylon. Daniel had been among the first taken, and nine years later, around 597 B.C., Ezekiel was taken. He remained there until at least 570 B.C.

The events therefore took place in and near Babylon, although Ezekiel described visions occurring elsewhere. Jeremiah and Daniel were contemporaries, and all three holy men may have known each other.

Note how carefully Ezekiel dated his visions.

DANIEL

Daniel means "God is my judge." It's an apt name. Daniel is one of the very few men in Scripture with whom the Bible finds absolutely no fault.

Combine Las Vegas with Rome and Paris, salt with additional opulence, and you'll have an idea of Babylon in her glory. Here was the most splendid city of the most powerful empire history had known to that time. Daniel was carried captive to Babylon at the time of the first deportation in 606 B.C. Because Babylon was of world importance under both Chaldeans and Persians, the positions Daniel attained in their governments were of world import. He was truly a big man in politics.

The last verse of chapter 5 is the understatement of the ages. With sixty miles of walls eighty feet thick, moats, and a crack army, Babylon was impregnable. She straddled the Euphrates river, half of her on each bank, and was thus assured of a constant water supply for the moats and the populace. During the wild party described in chapter 5, the Medes and Persians dammed the river upstream. They then walked down the riverbed and under the river gates into the heart of the city. The fall of the most spectacular empire of the age is summed up in one casual verse, 5:31.

HOSEA

Hosea means "salvation."

Following King Solomon's death the kingdom split into two politically separate factions—the Northern Kingdom, called Israel, and the Southern Kingdom, Judah. Note that Hosea made that distinction here, addressing most of his words to Israel. Samaria was the northern capital as Jerusalem was Judah's. At the split Judah kept the royal line of David but Israel's kings were not of David. Hosea alludes to that fact in 8:4.

Hosea ministered about 760-720 B.C., just before the Northern Kingdom was swept away by Assyria. Away back in Joshua the children of Israel had been ordered by God to wipe out every vestige of Canaanite religion. They didn't. Now the Northern Kingdom especially was as deep in the loathsome "worship" practices as Canaan ever had been. The religion crept into the life-style, of course, and the Israelites of Hosea's day were deeply immersed in the vilest, most degrading immoral practices imaginable. And they were supposed to be God's chosen.

Some commentators try to explain away the idea that Hosea married a harlot. After all...(ahem!). But plain language says he did. Moreover, it would have been difficult to find a young woman still pure, even a child bride. That's the moral condition Israel was in then.

JOEL

Joel means "Jahweh is God." He was among the earliest prophets, operating somewhere between 830 and 750 B.C. Most probably he lived around the time of King Joash. If the plague described by Joel was the same mentioned by Amos (Amos 4:9), then indeed he ministered earlier—800 B.C. or so.

"Assyria" and "Syria" were two completely different countries who had their heyday at two different times. Assyria lay east in the Tigris-Euphrates area. It was not a power to reckon with at the time of Joel. Syria lay more or less north of Israel. These were the aliens plaguing Israel at the time. The Greeks mentioned in 3:6 would not become a nation at all for another four hundred years at least.

"Valley of decision" (3:14) is a synonym for the Megiddo Valley lying up against Har-Megiddo, Armageddon.

AMOS

Amos means "burden-bearer." Amos dated his prophecy carefully, and Josephus says the earthquake would put it at 751 B.C. Within thirty years the Northern Kingdom would be swept away by the Assyrians. When Amos said the pampered ladies in 4:1-2 would be led away with hooks, he was being literal. The Assyrians set iron hooks in their captives' lips or jaws and led them about thus.

During Amos' ministry, the practices, religious and otherwise, of the Israelites were unspeakably filthy by any standard. Amos also spoke of her apostasy—that is, her turning away from God.

The "Jacob" in chapter 7 is another word for Israel—
remember that Jacob's name was changed to Israel by
God (Genesis 32:28 and 35:10). Samaria was capital of the
Northern Kingdom and the center of the idolatrous
worship.

OBADIAH

Obadiah means "servant or worshiper of the LORD."

Obadiah probably prophesied around 840-825 B.C., in
which case the plunder mentioned in 11-14 is the one by
Philistines and Arabs in 2 Chronicles 21:16-17.

Obadiah was speaking not to the Jews but to the nation
Edom. Edom was of the descent of Esau, Jacob's (Israel's)
brother back in Genesis 25:25-29. Edom and Israel were
usually at enmity with each other. The land of Edom lay
southeast of the Holy Land in a mountain fastness that
seemed impregnable. Edomites specialized in caravan-
robbing and other something-for-nothing schemes,
striking, then retreating to their rock clefts.

In Jesus' day Edom would be called Idumea. Herod the
Great and his descendants would be Idumean, not Jewish.

JONAH

This is the Jonah mentioned in 2 Kings 14:25. He
ministered during the reign of Jeroboam II, around 790-
720 B.C. If he preached to Nineveh early, its repentance
may have been the reason Israel restored some of her
borders in the 2 Kings passage. Gath-Hepher, Jonah's
hometown, is near Nazareth, where Jesus grew up. *Jonah*
means "dove."

Nineveh was capital of the Assyrian Empire. Not only
were the Assyrians powerful, they were land-hungry and
exceedingly cruel. They had been harassing Israel for
some years and were at the height of their power and
glory. Nineveh was literally the last place in the world

Jonah would want to see saved from destruction. Mercy to the brutal Assyrians? Perish the thought!

MICAH

Micah's full name was Micaiah (but not the Micaiah of 1 Kings 22:8), meaning "who is like Jahweh?"

The kingdom of Solomon had been split. Samaria was now capital of the Northern Kingdom, Israel. The kingly line was not of David. And the worship was an abominable mix of calf worship, Baal worship (featuring things like the sacrifice of babies and legal prostitution), and other Canaanite practices God forbade.

The Southern Kingdom, Judah, still kept the line of David on the throne and still maintained the Temple in Jerusalem, but Canaanite practices had infiltrated her also. Both kingdoms in God's eyes were ripe for judgment. Micah probably wrote around 740 B.C., before Samaria fell to the Assyrians. The book is best known for its "Thou, Bethlehem" quote that put the wise men on the trail of the King (Matthew 2:1-8). If portions of Micah sound a lot like parts of Isaiah, it may be that they were contemporaries and probably knew each other well.

NAHUM

Nahum means "comforter." He wrote probably somewhere around 650 B.C. Whereas Jonah preached to Nineveh a message of repentance, Nahum's was unvarnished doom. Zephaniah wrote at the same time.

Nineveh was capital of Assyria, a vicious and arrogant military empire. The city and its surrounding area were both protected and served by an extensive canal system. Twenty years or so after Nahum's oracle, the Babylonians and Medes joined forces against Nineveh. An unexpected flood washed away part of the river-gate defenses and provided the enemy with a way through the walls.

Nahum's word picture is a vivid description of the scene historians worked out.

HABAKKUK

Habakkuk means "soother" or "embracer." He wrote just before the fall of Jerusalem, say around 610 B.C.

The Assyrians had the reputation for cruelty, but the Babylonians were just about as bad. They, too, for instance, blinded captives and led them around with hooks thrust through the lips, jaw, or tongue. Babylon is the capital of the region called Chaldea and the two names, although not synonymous, are more or less interchangeable. Babylon and Nineveh had long been rivals, often enemies. Babylon destroyed Nineveh as well as Israel-Judah and not long afterwards Egypt, too. This made her queen of the earth but no less despicable in Habakkuk's eyes.

ZEPHANIAH

Zephaniah means "hidden or protected by Jahweh." He ministered during the reign of Josiah—somewhere around 639-608 B.C. and the siege of Jerusalem by Babylon commenced two years later. Manasseh (2 Chronicles 33), one of the wickedest of Judah's kings, had reinstated the vilest of Canaanite practices. When Josiah (2 Chronicles 34-35) brought in extensive reforms, Zephaniah was probably the voice behind the throne.

Baal and Milcom were Canaanite gods, forbidden to Jews.

The passage 2:4-7 all refers to the Philistines, Israel's old nemesis. True to 2:5, they are no more. Moab-Ammon (2:8-11) was the land on the east side of the Jordan River; Israel of course lay on the west. They, too, were ancient enemies. Assyria (2:13-15) was past her prime but still the enemy who had wiped out the Northern Kingdom and had come very near to destroying Jerusalem. Scholars say 3:1 and on refer to Jerusalem rather than Nineveh because it says "her God," singular, and Assyria worshiped a plurality of gods.

HAGGAI

Haggai means "festive" or "celebration." He was mentioned by Ezra (Ezra 5:1; 6:14) and ministered around 520 B.C., give or take. The date in 1:1 is probably June 1, 520 B.C. Haggai, incidentally, ministered about the time of Confucius and Buddha.

The book explains how the Temple, razed by the Babylonians, was being rebuilt—and the problems the builders had to buck. Haggai was in the midst of this. The new Temple was a pallid imitation of the former, glorious, Temple of Solomon. Jewish writers say it lacked the Shekinah glory, holy fire, the Ark of the Covenant, Urim and Thummin (by which priests ascertained the will of God), and a spirit of prophecy. This new Temple would be extensively rebuilt and refurbished by Jesus' day.

The Persians, conquerors of Babylon, were now the masters of the Jews. Zechariah (the next book following), a younger prophet, was Haggai's contemporary.

ZECHARIAH

Zechariah means "Jahweh remembers." He and Haggai ministered about the same time toward, in part, the same ends—edification of the Jews and building the Temple. Babylonia and Assyria had both risen and fallen, taking the Jews down with them. Now Persia (with the aid of the Medes) was in command of the Near East. Jerusalem, devastated for seventy years, was being repopulated as the Jews trickled back into their land out of exile, picking up the pieces.

The cubit in chapter 5 was probably about eighteen

inches, making the scroll fifteen feet by thirty feet. The "fourth year of Darius" in 7:1 would be 518 B.C. by most reckoning.

The cities and regions in chapter 9 are listed in an interesting order. About two hundred years later, in 332 B.C., Alexander the Great would come through, conquering them in exactly the order given. But he spared Jerusalem.

MALACHI

Malachi's full name was "Malachiah," meaning "messenger of Jahweh." His book is taken by nearly all authorities to be God's final word until the appearance of the Messiah four hundred years later. Malachi ministered around 450-400 B.C., probably. The book of Nehemiah explains the history of Malachi's day. The Jews were settling back into their homeland after exile and dispersion. Much would happen to them in the next four hundred years. Already the warnings against impurity were starting. Incidentally, note that there is no warning against false gods. The Jews went down because of their Canaanite practices, but they came home staunch monotheists.

THE NEW TESTAMENT

A lot happened between the testaments, especially in the political sphere. These shifts are shown in the time chart in Appendix B. Babylon, Assyria, and Persia were forgotten in the shadow of Rome. If ever God's people could use a Messiah, it was now!

THE GOSPELS

These four accounts of the life of Jesus Christ were accepted as authoritative from the very beginning of the church. They frame what we know of His Person.

MATTHEW

Matthew ("gift of Jahweh"), also named Levi, lived in Capernaum near the north shore of the Sea of Galilee. He was a tax collector, despised by Roman and Jew alike.

The internal structure and allusions suggest that this gospel was written for the Jews in particular. It even makes use of certain mnemonic tricks employed in Jewish schools. The date: before A.D. 70, probably between 56 and 60. It is not altogether chronological in its details of Jesus' life and thus differs from the other gospels.

Of interest: There are four women besides Mary in the genealogy, chapter 1. Look them up in Genesis 38, Joshua 2 and 6, Ruth, and 2 Samuel 11 and 12. In a concordance use key words to look up in the Old Testament those passages about which Jesus said, "Have you not read?" or Matthew says, "Thus it is written," and so forth.

MARK

This Mark was probably John Mark. John=Johanan ("grace of God") was his Jewish name, Marcus his Roman name. Earliest tradition makes this the first of the gospels written—near A.D. 50. Mark was putting down Peter's account, essentially. And probably this book was for Romans (perhaps written in Rome). Many Jewish words, places, and customs are explained—not necessary for a Jewish readership. Mark grew up in Jerusalem. His mother was an influential convert. It was her house Peter headed for in Acts 12:12.

Of interest: Note how often Mark uses "immediately" or "straightway." Mark alone mentions the incident in 14:51-52. Was that he himself?

LUKE

Luke, or Lucas (short for Lucanus, meaning "light-giving"), had no alternative Jewish name. He was the only Gentile New Testament writer. But his gospel plus Acts is longer than the work of any Jewish writer's. He was a physician, an educated man of means. Close traveling companion of Paul, he also knew Jesus' mother, Mary, personally as well as the other apostles and a lot of the first-century Christian leaders. He got around. Apparently he was born in Antioch of Syria; his language and life-style were quite cultured. He was with Paul during that apostle's imprisonment in Caesarea (A.D. 58 to 60) and probably wrote this gospel then, when he had access to both people and other writings.

Of interest: Luke's unique mentions of women here and there; his attention to little medical details; the many details he must have obtained directly from Mary.

JOHN

John (Johanan = "gift or grace of Jahweh") is the apostle John who, with James his brother, left his father's fishing fleet to fish for men with Jesus. By custom of the day a woman needed a man over her. When Jesus faced His death, he transferred His responsibility to protect Mary (as firstborn son) to John (John 19:25-27). Some time after Pentecost (in Acts 2), John moved from the Holy Land to Ephesus (on the Aegean coast of modern Turkey). He was long the special friend of Peter.

John probably wrote this gospel sometime around A.D. 95, well after the other three gospels were in circulation. Only eight percent of John's gospel is repeated in the others—the rest is new material. His gospel dovetails especially with Luke's, as if he were writing major things Luke hadn't gotten to.

Tradition says John was the only apostle who lived to a ripe old age (but not because his persecutors wanted him to; tradition also says he was dumped into boiling oil and emerged unharmed). While exiled on Patmos he wrote Revelation (Apocalypse). He was also author of the three letters called "John."

Of interest: The wonderful way he used a limited vocabulary of common words, as in the first few sentences.

HISTORY

ACTS OF THE APOSTLES

Scholars agree that Acts was almost certainly written by Luke. Since it closes with Paul in Rome the date was probably close to A.D. 63. The book itself is its own historical background. You will find a map helpful for tracing journeys and locating nations. By reading Paul's itineraries carefully you can just about pick out where he was when he wrote each letter that was to become part of our New Testament.

Of interest: Watch how often Paul (1) entered a new town's synagogue, (2) got booted out by the Jews, (3) took up residence close by, and (4) converted Gentiles before being driven off by the Jews who followed him about. Note, too, where Luke entered the picture by changing the narrative from third person (he, they) to first (we). What a remarkable array of fascinating characters this book contains!

PAUL'S LETTERS

ROMANS

Paul wrote this letter from Corinth in A.D. 58. He had not yet visited the church at Rome, though he knew some of the believers there. This carefully framed epistle (epistle is a fancy word for "letter") is called the Constitution of the Church because it outlines the major points of doctrine. Note that it begins with those who had never been formally introduced to God and ends with the church itself. Most of the believers in Rome were Gentiles, apparently, rather than Jews.

1 CORINTHIANS

This letter, written to Corinth from Paul in Ephesus around A.D. 56, points up what other historians have verified—the church at Corinth was sitting in a moral cesspool. In vernacular Greek, to act like a Corinthian was to be practicing fornication. Corinth was a major port with its attendant waterfront taverns and shady businesses. About fifty miles from Athens on the Greek coast, it contained maybe four hundred thousand people. The great temple of Aphrodite (goddess of love) was staffed with 1000 prostitutes.

Paul had founded the church there about three years earlier. He had written at least one and possibly several letters (now lost) to her believers since then. Now he had received word of several problems and lapses of moral behavior and was writing to correct them before his next visit.

2 CORINTHIANS

(See 1 Corinthians for background.) The problems at Corinth seemed, in the main, to be straightened out. Considering the general depravity of the city, that was no small accomplishment. Now Paul was writing again to commend them for shaping up their act and to reaffirm his position as apostle. This letter more than any other peeks into Paul's complex personality. He was hardly your "mild-mannered reporter for a great metropolitan newspaper."

GALATIANS

Galatia was, more or less, the heart of what is now Turkey in Asia Minor. Paul wrote his letter somewhere between A.D. 49 and 55. Unlike Rome or Corinth, Galatia consisted of a lot of little towns; probably it was mostly farm country. Paul touched the area on all three of his missionary journeys.

The letter in large part was an answer to Judaizers. Some claimed that to accept the Jewish Messiah, Jesus, you had to take on the trappings of the Jews—circumcision, and so on. The Galatians were even keeping the Jewish holidays in their enthusiasm to do things right.

EPHESIANS

Ephesus was blessed with leaders. Priscilla and Aquila were there. Paul spent years there. Timothy worked there and the apostle John probably wrote his gospel there. He made the city his headquarters. The temple of Artemis (Diana) was at Ephesus, and the making of statues of Diana was one of the city's major industries. Since Ephesus was a major trade port, marketing these souvenirs was never a problem, either. Acts 19 tells of one of Paul's missionary visits and of the amusing near-riot the craftsmen caused.

Paul wrote this letter around A.D. 61 and probably intended that it be circulated generally among churches (which it was).

PHILIPPIANS

Macedonia was the northern part of what we call Greece. Alexander the Great, who founded the Greek Empire, was a Macedonian. His father, Philip, founded a small city. This was it—Philippi. Luke may have practiced medicine here—in fact, he may even have either been from here or lived here a long time. The church at Philippi, founded by Paul ten years before this letter was written, was one of the solidest and straightest.

Now it was A.D. 61 and Paul was imprisoned at Rome. Philippi had sent him a gift of money, and this was his thank-you letter (among other things, of course).

COLOSSIANS

Colossae had been a trade center for centuries, lying on a main road across what is now Turkey (about one hundred miles east of the coastal trade city of Ephesus). Now its importance as a city had drastically declined. The Colossians were a curious mix of Greeks, Romans, and Asiatics, and their thinking showed it. Tending to rely on their own philosophies, they mixed heretical ideas into the gospel. This letter by Paul, written around A.D. 61 when he was in a Roman prison, was designed to set the Colossians straight about their Christ. Historians doubt that Paul ever visited Colossae himself, although he passed nearby several times.

1 AND 2 THESSALONIANS

Paul visited Thessalonica on both his second and third missionary journeys. Acts 17:1-15 tells his problems there. While at Athens, Paul, anxious for the welfare of his fledgling church there, wrote back to the Thessalonians. The date of the first letter, then, is A.D. 51. Not long thereafter, he sent the second letter to clear up a few little questions about when the end was coming.

Thessalonica, or Salonika, was a coastal city in Macedonia, the northern part of Greece. It was not far from Philippi and also Berea. Note Paul's comment about Thessalonica and Berea in Acts 17:11.

PAUL'S PASTORAL EPISTLES

"Pastoral epistles" is fancy talk for the letters Paul wrote to Timothy and Titus, ministers, or pastors, in the new churches.

1 TIMOTHY

(See 2 Timothy.) Paul had left Timothy in Ephesus in Asia Minor to build up that church. Now Paul had been detained up in Macedonia and was writing Timothy a letter of instruction and encouragement. The date may have been somewhere around A.D. 63 before Paul's imprisonment.

2 TIMOTHY

Luke was a buddy; Peter was an apostolic friend. But it was Timothy who warmed Paul's heart most. Timothy and Paul were so unalike, too. Paul was mercurial, Timothy rock steady. Paul had studied under the renowned teacher

Gamaliel. Timothy's teachers were his Jewish mother and grandma. Paul argued nose-to-nose with Peter and then warned Timothy not to talk back in an unseemly way.

Now Paul saw his death in the near future. And it was Timothy he longed for. "Make every effort to come to me soon (4:9, NASB)."*

Paul's imminent martyrdom places the date around A.D. 66.

TITUS

Paul probably wrote this letter to Titus about the same time he wrote 1 Timothy, around A.D. 63. Titus is mentioned in various places as having been with Paul. With two others he carried Paul's second letter to the Corinthians. He worked extensively on the Greek island of Crete, and in 2 Timothy is mentioned as having gone to Dalmatia (what is now Yugoslavia, across the water from Italy).

PHILEMON

Talk about tact! Paul was in prison in Rome, about A.D. 63. Now the slave of his good friend Philemon in Colossae had run away. Somehow the slave ended up with Paul in Rome and had become a convert to the gospel. Paul now had a runaway slave who had become a Christian brother to both Paul and the master. This was the letter the slave, Onesimus, carried with him when he returned to obey the master he had left.

Onesimus was on dangerous ground indeed, returning. A runaway was subject to the death penalty. Onesimus had stolen money from his master in addition. It took courage to go back.

Did Philemon receive his slave back without harming him? Did he free the slave as Paul's hint (v.21) suggested he ought to do? Tradition says he did and that Onesimus

*New American Standard Bible.

ended up a bishop in Berea.

The name *Onesimus* means "useful" or "beneficial." Paul made a pun on the name three times—twice in verse 11, once in 20.

HEBREWS

Some say Paul wrote Hebrews. Others claim no. The best date figured out is between A.D. 64 and 68, just before the Romans leveled Jerusalem in 70. James had been murdered around 63, and the church at Jerusalem was in turmoil. Worse years lay ahead. The mention of Timothy in 13:23 also suggests that time. If Paul did write it, is it not reasonable that he failed to associate his name with it? Among the Jews in Jerusalem his name was mud and wouldn't help the cause of the letter at all.

This letter seems directed to Jews who had become converts to Christ Jesus—thus the title.

GENERAL EPISTLES

These are letters named after their respective writers and addressed to Christian churches in general.

JAMES

There are several Jameses in Scripture. Two were among the twelve apostles; James son of Zebedee and James son of Alphaeus. The oldest half-brother of Jesus was also a James (Matthew 13:55), and it is believed this writer was that brother. If he is, Jesus appeared to him specifically after His resurrection (1 Corinthians 15:7). This is one of the earliest letters in the New Testament, dating perhaps around A.D. 50.

1 AND 2 PETER

Ah, Peter. From a headstrong, overconfident, foul-mouthed fisherman, Peter mellowed into one of the strongest and gentlest of our Lord's apostles. This was indeed the Simon (given name) Peter (or Cephas, meaning "rock") of the gospels. He was the Cephas mentioned in Galatians 2:11.

These two letters by Peter to the churches in general were probably written around A.D. 65 or 66. At that time Nero was executing his persecutions against the Christians in and around Rome.

1, 2, AND 3 JOHN
The John who wrote these letters is the same John who wrote the gospel of John and the Revelation, or Apocalypse.

John probably wrote these letters late in his ministry and probably while he was in Ephesus. The identity of "the elect lady" is unkown—various guesses range from the suggestion that it was a particular lady in whose home a church met, or that it is the church, Christ's bride.

JUDE
Jude, or Judas, was most likely also Jesus' half-brother (Matthew 13:55). This was not, of course, the apostle Judas. The letter was probably written around A.D. 67. This was the time Nero burned Rome and intensified his deliberate persecution of Christians.

REVELATION
The second great persecution of the church was in full swing in A.D. 95 under the Roman emperor Domitian. The apostle John had been boiled in oil and survived. He was next exiled to the little island of Patmos, not really too far from Ephesus. He returned to the Asia Minor mainland in A.D. 96. Whether he wrote his vision when he saw it (95) or when he returned (96) matters little.

The seven churches mentioned are clustered together near the west coast of Asia Minor and were in John's immediate governing area.

Appendix B

THE CHRONOLOGY OF SCRIPTURE

The further back into history historians dig, the shakier precise dates become. Different authorities—and excellent ones, too—add up figures the best they can and come out with wholly different dates. Was the Exodus in 1400 B.C. or in 1250 B.C.?

Although precise figures vary, the chronology itself— that is, the order in which things happen—is uniform.

The dates given here, then, are to be taken with a grain of salt. They will give you the general idea of when who was doing what to whom. The events themselves, not the dates, carry the lessons for us.

The books themselves, when mentioned, are in italics.

Dates approximate

c. 4000 B.C.	Adam, according to calculations by Bishop Ussher (Genesis 2)
c. 2000 B.C.	Abraham, Isaac, and Jacob (Genesis 12-35)
c. 1800 B.C.	Israel, under Joseph's aegis, went to Egypt (Genesis 46). Egyptians enslaved the Hebrews; period of *Genesis* closed (Exodus 1).
c. 1450 B.C.	Moses led the Exodus (Exodus 3-15) and wrote Pentateuch. Period of the *Exodus*
c. 1400 B.C.	Israel crossed Jordan and began conquest of Canaan. Period of *Joshua*
c. 1400-1100 B.C.	Period of the *Judges*. *Ruth* lived during this time.

c. 1050 B.C.	*Samuel* anointed Saul king of Israel; he would reign forty years (1 Samuel 9-10).
c. 1000 B.C.	David became king of Judah; he was made king of all Israel 7½ years later (2 Samuel 2, 5).
973-933 B.C.	Solomon became king (965-926?); he, too, would reign forty years (1 Kings 1).
970 B.C.	Solomon built the great Temple; it would stand nearly four hundred years (1 Kings 5-8).
960 B.C.	*Song of Solomon*
940 B.C.	*Ecclesiastes* probably written; *Proverbs* assembled during Solomon's time and shortly thereafter.
933 B.C.	Solomon died; the kingdom split into Israel in the north, Judah in the south (1 Kings 11:43—12:19).
933-916 B.C.	Rehoboam reigned in Judah (1 Kings 12).
933-911 B.C.	Jeroboam reigned in Israel (1 Kings 12).
915-913 B.C.	Abijah reigned in Judah (1 Kings 15:1).
912-872 B.C.	Asa reigned in Judah (1 Kings 15:9).
911-910 B.C.	Nadab reigned in Israel (1 Kings 14:20; 15:25).
910-887 B.C.	Baasha reigned in Israel (1 Kings 15:27-34).
887-886 B.C.	Elah was king of Israel (1 Kings 16:6).
886 B.C.	Zimri reigned seven days (1 Kings 16:15).
886-875 B.C.	Omri ruled as king of Israel (1 Kings 16:21-28).

875-850 B.C.	Elijah the prophet ministered, primarily to Israel (1 Kings 17-19, 21, etc.).
875-854 B.C.	Ahab ruled Israel; his wife, Jezebel, introduced further idolatrous worship (1 Kings 16:29—22:40).
874-850 B.C.	Jehoshaphat ruled Judah (1 Kings 22:41).
855-854 B.C.	Ahaziah reigned over Israel (2 Kings 22:51).
854-843 B.C.	Joram ruled in Israel (2 Kings 1:17).
850-843 B.C.	Jehoram ruled in Judah (1 Kings 22:50).
850-800 B.C.	The ministry of Elisha the prophet (2 Kings 2).
843 B.C.	Ahaziah ruled one year in Judah; his mother was Athaliah (2 Kings 8:25—9:28).
843-837 B.C.	Athaliah usurped the throne as Judah's only queen after killing nearly all the seed of David (2 Kings 11).
843-816 B.C.	Jehu ruled over Israel following a bloody takeover (2 Kings 9).
843-803 B.C.	Joash, sole survivor of Athaliah's slaughter, was put on the throne of Judah at the age of seven (also spelled Jehoash) (2 Kings 11).
840-825 B.C.	Ministry of Obadiah the prophet
825-811 B.C.	Joel recorded his prophecies.
820-804 B.C.	Jehoahaz ruled in Israel (2 Kings 13).
804-790 B.C.	Joash ruled in Israel (2 Kings 13:10).

803-775 B.C.	Amaziah ruled in Judah; he brought down Edom by taking Petra (Sela) and killing 10,000 Edomites in the Dead Sea rift (2 Kings 14).
790-749 B.C.	Jeroboam II ruled in Israel (2 Kings 14).
787-735 B.C.	Uzziah, also called Azariah, ruled Judah; coregent, he was a leper (2 Kings 14:21; 15).
784-772 B.C.	*Jonah* prophesied to Nineveh, served in the court of Judah (dates may have been 810-802).
776 B.C.	First Olympiad in Greece, marking its beginning as an entity.
765-755 B.C.	*Amos* prophesied (may have been 780-740).
760-713 B.C.	*Isaiah*
755-713 B.C.	*Hosea*
749-734 B.C.	Jotham ruled in Judah (2 Kings 15:32).
748 B.C.	Zechariah ruled Israel six months (2 Kings 15).
748 B.C.	Shallum ruled one month, was overthrown (2 Kings 15:13).
748-738 B.C.	Menahem overthrew Shallum, ruled Israel (2 Kings 15:14).
741-726 B.C.	Ahaz ruled in Judah (2 Kings 16).
737-735 B.C.	Pekahiah ruled in Israel (2 Kings 15:23).
735-715 B.C.	Pekah ruled Israel coregent with others? (2 Kings 15:27).

734 B.C.	Tiglath-pileser of Assyria took over a chunk of northern Israel (2 Kings 15:29).
733-700 B.C.	*Micah* prophesied.
730 B.C.	Judah under Ahaz commenced paying tribute to Tiglath-pileser of Assyria (2 Kings 16:7-8).
730-721 B.C.	Hoshea usurped the throne of Israel (2 Kings 17).
726-697 B.C.	Hezekiah reigned over Judah, partly coregent with Ahaz (2 Kings 18-20).
722 B.C.	Assyria carried away all the kingdom of Israel; Assyria came to the walls of Jerusalem and turned aside (2 Kings 18-19).
697-642 B.C.	Manasseh reigned in Judah, reinstated Canaanite practices (2 Kings 21).
650-620 B.C.	*Nahum* prophesied the fall of Nineveh.
641-639 B.C.	Amon ruled in Judah (2 Kings 21:19).
640 B.C.	*Zephaniah* wrote his prophecies.
639-608 B.C.	Josiah became king of Judah, initiated far-flung reforms (2 Kings 22).
626 B.C.	The Scythians invaded Assyria, beginning its downfall.
626-575 B.C.	*Jeremiah,* the weeping prophet, watched Judah go down.
620-609 B.C.	*Habakkuk*
617 B.C.	Conquest of Assyria by Babylon commenced.

612 or 607 B.C.	Nineveh fell to the Babylonians; Assyria was no more.
608 B.C.	Josiah died at Megiddo (2 Kings 23:28-30);Jehoahaz ruled three months, was exiled by Neco, Pharaoh of Egypt (2 Kings 23:31-33).
608-597 B.C.	Jehoiakim took the throne of Judah (2 Kings 23:34—24:6).
606 B.C.	First stage in the fall of Jerusalem. Babylon entered the city, pillaged the Temple and took captives (including, probably, Daniel) to Chaldea (2 Kings 24:15).
605 B.C.	Carchemish—Neco of Egypt met Babylonian forces in this battle that spelled the end of Egyptian supremacy and resulted in the supremacy of Babylon.
597 B.C.	Jehoiachin was king of Judah three months (2 Kings 24:8).
597-586 B.C.	Zedekiah was king of Judah (2 Kings 24).
597 B.C.	Ezekiel probably carried to Babylon.
593-560 B.C.	*Ezekiel* the prophet; visions probably occurred 592-587.
586 B.C.	The final destruction of Jerusalem. Judah was now desolate (2 Kings 25).
586? B.C.	*Obadiah*
538 B.C.	Babylon fell, conquered by the Persians and Medes (Daniel 5:30-31).

Appendix B

536 B.C.	Jews returned under Persian aegis and commenced rebuilding the Temple (Ezra 1).
536-516 B.C.	Zerubbabel, with Joshua, ruled in Jerusalem (Ezra).
520-505 B.C.	*Haggai*
520-490 B.C.	*Zechariah* the prophet
516 B.C.	The second Temple was completed (Ezra 6:15).
478 B.C.	*Esther* became queen of Persia (Esther 2:17).
473 B.C.	The Jews were saved in Persia through Esther's intercession (Esther 9).
458-457 B.C.	*Ezra* went to Jerusalem (Ezra 7).
445-436 B.C.	*Nehemiah* rebuilt wall of Jerusalem (Nehemiah 2:11—6:15).
435-415 B.C	*Malachi* prophesied.
332 B.C.	Palestine invaded by the Greeks under Alexander. He spared Jerusalem, intending to refurbish it.
323 B.C.	Alexander the Great died.
168 B.C.	Antiochus Epiphanes (175-164) defiled the Temple, enflaming Jewish rebellion.
167 B.C.	The Maccabean revolt
165 B.C.	Judas Maccabeus took Jerusalem, rededicated the Temple; the Holy Land would now be autonomous until the Roman conquest.

63 B.C.	Pompey made the Holy Land part of Roman Empire; Rome would still rule, with Herod as king, when Jesus was born.
5 or 4 B.C.	Jesus born in Bethlehem (Matthew 2; Luke 2).
8	Jesus visited Herod's Temple at Passover, age 12 (Luke 2:41-52).
26	Jesus began his formal ministry with baptism; this ministry would last apparently 3½ years (John 1:29-34).
30	Jesus was crucified (Mark 15). He is risen! (Mark 16). The church was established (Acts 2).
44	James son of Zebedee martyred (Acts 12:2).
45-48	Paul's first missionary journey (Acts 13)
49 or 55	*Galatians* was written.
50-53	Paul's second missionary journey (Acts 15:36—18:22)
50 or 51	*James* wrote his epistle.
50-56?	*Mark* wrote his gospel under Peter.
51	Paul wrote *1 and 2 Thessalonians*.
54-57	Paul's third missionary journey (Acts 18:24—21:17)
56?	*Matthew* wrote his gospel. Paul wrote *1 Corinthians*.
56-57	Paul wrote second letter to *Corinthians*.

56-58	Paul wrote to *Romans.*
58	Paul arrested in Jerusalem (Acts 21:33).
58-60	Paul spent two years under arrest in Caesarea (Acts 25-26).
58-60	*Luke* probably wrote his gospel.
60-61	Paul was taken to Rome for trial (Acts 27:1—28:15).
61-63	Paul wrote *Philemon, Colossians, Philippians,* and *Ephesians; Luke* wrote *Acts of the Apostles.*
63	Paul wrote first letter to *Timothy.* Paul was apparently acquitted in Rome and released.
64-68	*Hebrews* was written.
65	*Titus*
65-66	*Peter* wrote his letters.
66	Paul wrote a second time to *Timothy.*
66 or 67	Paul was beheaded in Rome, according to tradition.
67	*Jude* wrote his general epistle.
70	Jerusalem destroyed by Titus, many Jews enslaved.
73	Masada, last stronghold of Jewish resistance, fell to Rome; Israel was again erased as a nation.
90-95	*John* wrote his gospel.
90-95	John wrote his three letters *(1, 2, 3 John).*

95-96   John wrote his *Revelation,* or
                 Apocalypse.

150   The New Testament as we know it
                 began taking shape.

Moody Press, a ministry of the Moody Bible
Institute, is designed for education, evangelization,
and edification. If we may assist you in knowing
more about Christ and the Christian life, please
write us without obligation: Moody Press, c/o
MLM, Chicago, Illinois 60610.